A LANE COUNTY

ALMANAC

10mm 20 30 40 50

Northwest Botanical Institute
David H. Wagner, Ph.D.
Research and Analysis
Training and Consulting

P.O. Box 30064
Eugene, OR 97403 U.S. A.
davidwagner@mac.com

A Lane County ALMANAC

By David H. Wagner

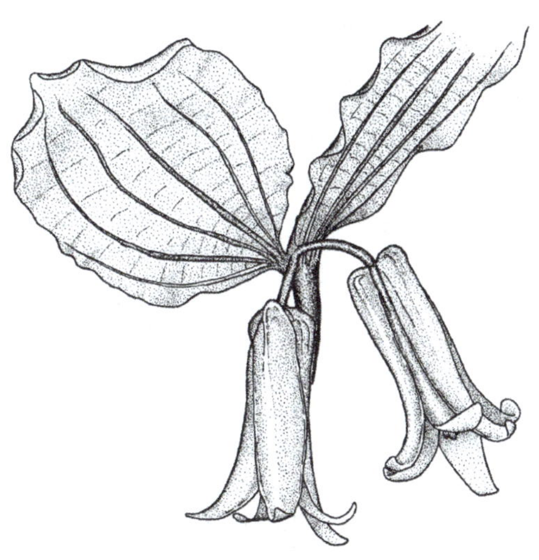

Edited with an Introduction by
William L. Sullivan

Published by the Northwest Botanical Institute
PO Box 30064
Eugene, Oregon 97403

Contents

To Anita Johnson,

a lifelong journalist who is passionate about her work. In retirement she and two colleagues bought Eugene Weekly, *turning it into an outstanding alternative newspaper. She recruited me to write a monthly illustrated nature column. Those columns form the core of this Almanac.*

Introduction

David Wagner is that rare scientist with the gift to bridge worlds, sharing his love for nature in a way everyone can understand. In the scientific community he may be acclaimed as Oregon's leading expert on liverworts, mosses, and ferns. But the rest of us are more likely to know him as the author of the *Oregon Nature Calendar* and *Eugene Weekly*'s "It's About Time" column.

Wagner's writings have become popular not merely for his useful tips about gardening and birdwatching, but because he includes fascinating trivia from the natural world. He tells us why the male and female flowers of bigleaf maples bloom at different times. Did you know that garter snakes bear live young in the third week of August?

Wagner was born in Michigan but he grew up in India, where his parents were Methodist missionaries. His love of the outdoors blosomed at a boarding school in the foothills of the Himalayas, where he spent nine months each year from kindergarten through high school.

When Wagner returned to the U.S. for college, he chose the University of Puget Sound because mountains were nearby, and "I was in love with the mountains." He earned his Ph.D in botany at Washington State University, writing a dissertation on ferns.

Straight out of college, he accepted a job as curator and director of the University of Oregon Herbarium in 1976. His first spring in

Eugene, he resolved to learn the local flora by taking a walk once a week along the Willamette River in Alton Baker Park, across a footbridge from the university. Soon he was leading weekly nature walks on the route, free to anyone who showed up Thursday at noon. That weekly tradition continued seventeen years, allowing him to catalog the effect of our changing climate on the blooming times of native plants.

Wagner influenced a generation of UO students with his Systematic Botany classes. He was instrumental in building the Mount Pisgah Arboretum into an outdoor educational institution. As president of the Eugene Natural History Society he wrote countless essays, many of them collected here.

And yet this fascinating, approachable scientist says that he always felt he was an outsider. As a boy he was the only one in his school who hiked alone in the Himalayas at night. When he was hired to map rare plants for the Bureau of Land Management he worked in the woods for a week at a time from spring to fall, staying at budget motels where he learned to bring his own light bulbs. Even then, he would spend at least three days a year camping in the wilderness alone.

If loving the natural world makes a person an "outsider," count me in. With his writings, David Wagner has bridged a bigger gap than he perhaps knows, revealing that the world is a kaleidoscope of marvels, and that we have permission to gaze at it in astonishment.

– William L. Sullivan
Eugene, Oregon

PART ONE

Month By Month in Lane County

In winter, Canada geese rest on submerged logs at the Delta Ponds.

January

One of the reasons I love this region, and Eugene in particular, is that our winters are friendly. I sometimes even say we have no winter, that we have a rainy season stitching fall and spring together. On almost any day we can take a walk without struggling with the elements. Even when it snows, as is happening as I write this, the storm is transitory.

Today the hawks are perched in the trees to hunt and the herons are keeping vigil by the neighborhood ponds to fish. In the ponds Canada geese tend to sit very still this time of the year. They seem to be in deep meditation as they rest on logs. Coots and grebes, on the other hand, are always swimming about or diving. Tree frogs are starting to croak. More like "creeeeek," actually. I think they are just warming up their vocal cords. The robust friggetting hasn't yet started.

The plant world is active, too. The big herbaceous perennial leaves coming out of the ground are poison hemlock. Seedlings of winter annuals are well past the cotyledon stage. Mosses on the fence have grown their spore capsules tall enough that spores are developing inside. The spores themselves won't disperse until the weather warms up and the capsules dry out.

Along my daily walking route I notice that two lichen colonies on a rock wall are bigger than my hand. Over the past years I've watch them grow from disks only about two inches across. Now the two colonies are starting to merge. What a fine project it would be to take a picture of this rock every January and document the lichens' growth!

* * *

The wind was blustering across the top of Gillespie Butte when I pulled my wife close and gave her a sudden kiss. "What brought that on?" she asked. "Look up," I replied. "We're under the mistletoe."

The old oak trees on the top of Gillespie Butte, near our home in North Eugene, have mistletoe on their gnarly branches. Their branches stand out strongly this time of the year, naked nearly two months now and to remain exposed like this until spring is well under way. Oak trees with swollen, twisted branches are admired as icons of toughness and durability. One on Gillespie Butte has been designated a legacy tree by the Eugene

Our oaks have gnarly branches because they are fighting parasitic mistletoe.

Tree Foundation. However, there are oaks much older than this legacy tree that don't show this kind of tortured branching, but instead show rather graceful, wavy, upward forking patterns.

It is the mistletoe that causes the gnarly character of our oaks. Mistletoe is a stem parasite, sending probing, absorptive organs called haustoria into the living tissue of the oak branches. These haustoria take the place of roots for mistletoe, sucking water and nutrients from the oak host. The oak responds by attempting to smother the roots in masses of woody scar tissue. The lumps and twists in the branches grow at the sites of these parasitic infections, squeezing off their nutrient supply. The very few vestiges of mistletoe that occasionally persist on old infection burls prove that smothering works. Only near the tips of branches, where mistletoe infections are young, do you see large clumps of vigorous mistletoe.

* * *

Migration is the word for January. The ponds and reservoirs in the valley are teeming with winter residents. Nothing makes nice binoculars pay off more than feasting the eyes on the intricate patterns of a male green-winged teal, shoveler, or bufflehead. I never get over the flash of amazement at how quickly a bufflehead can spin over and disappear under the water on a dive. Similarly startling is a cormorant suddenly coming up like a submarine periscope breaking a glassy surface.

Northern shovelers overwinter in Oregon.

Out at the coast another migration is under way. Gray whales are passing southbound in early January at rates reaching thirty individuals per hour. Promontories like Yaquina Head are excellent viewing spots. Many coastal overlooks will have volunteer naturalists providing information about the whales. The next big wave of migration will be in May when the cows and calves pass northward.

* * *

"A fitful watch I kept of sleep's domain; the wintry night was wracked by wind and rain ..."

When lines like these come to me in my dreams and it is dark when I wake up, it must be January.

The days are getting longer, but the change from day to day is not easily noticed. Nine hours from sunrise to sunset at the beginning of the month, nine hours and 35 minutes at the end of the month. Another month when the most exciting events play out very slowly, hidden from view.

Buffleheads spin and dive in a flash.

Beaver breeding season begins this month; it peaks in early February. Beaver kits are born sixteen weeks later. Black bear mating season was way back in June and July. After fertilization, the embryos developed very slowly and were implanted only last month. Then fetuses grow at a fantastic rate, and babies are delivered late this month or early February. The bears are hibernating in dens under logs or ancient stumps; their cubs' emergence into the wild is yet some time away.

Few other members of our fauna hibernate. Seeing a red-eared slider out sunning himself on the third of January taught me a new word: brumation. These reptiles do not hibernate, they brumate, coming out when there is a sudden warm spell but burrowing back into the mud when it gets cold again. It makes me wonder if I should brumate the rest of winter.

One December the east Delta Ponds froze and then seven inches of snow fell, making for a rare and beautiful scene. When the snow melted on a single warm day, the ponds revealed dozens of patches of tapering, branching, clear lines radiating outwards from one point. These patterns were evenly spread across the ponds, three to ten feet in diameter, over inch-thick ice. The mechanism behind the formation of these patterns is a topic of debate among my geophysical friends.

A humorous scene was created by a nutria moseying across the ice. Its tail left a wavy line in the snow as if a big snake had crossed the pond. Footprints in each crook of the wavy lane gave it away as an animal track. Almost as funny were two Canada geese standing on the ice, seemingly unclear on the concept of ice. The frozen ponds were otherwise devoid of bird life. All the ducks, cormorants, and other geese had taken refuge across the highway, in ponds where a river current keeps open water available.

Red-eared sliders don't hibernate. They brumate, sunning when it's warm.

You can tell that western pocket gophers don't hibernate. Their mounds pooch up even in this freezing weather. They will start breeding in February to produce litters in March.

* * *

Botanists have an advantage this time of year because they can sense spring coming. True, with the solstice just behind us, most of the official winter is still ahead. Yet buds on the leafless trees and shrubs are swelling, noticeably increasing in size from week to week. The woodland herbs are emerging from the ground, splashes of bright green. As long as it is above freezing, light is the limiting variable for plants, not temperature. The evergreens are photosynthesizing, sap is rising, and the buds swelling.

Those who only watch birds don't have it as good. It is indeed a treat to watch the shovelers and buffleheads cruise around the Delta Ponds, displaying their tidy swimming style. They will leave when spring arrives but there's no way to tell when that might occur just by watching the birds. I'm sure the birds, like the botanists, watch the buds swell and the herbs proliferate. We all wait for the days' lengthening.

Our climate is so mild that few animals hibernate. The animals that remain active often work hard to find food this time of the year. Elk move into lowland forests and eat lichens. River otters can be seen in urban ponds. Birds forage in flocks that include pine siskins from the mountains.

In the plant world, the swelling buds on the willows, cottonwoods, and osoberries sing a song of glee. Low groundwater levels from last summer's dry spell are being replenished. A surprise to a botanist is how long the snowberries hang onto their fruit. The berries are aptly named, practically glowing white at the tips of slender dark branches. They are one of the few decorations in the valley woodlands this time of year. Snowberries must be distasteful to birds, to remain so long. Maybe they are starvation food, the last to be eaten?

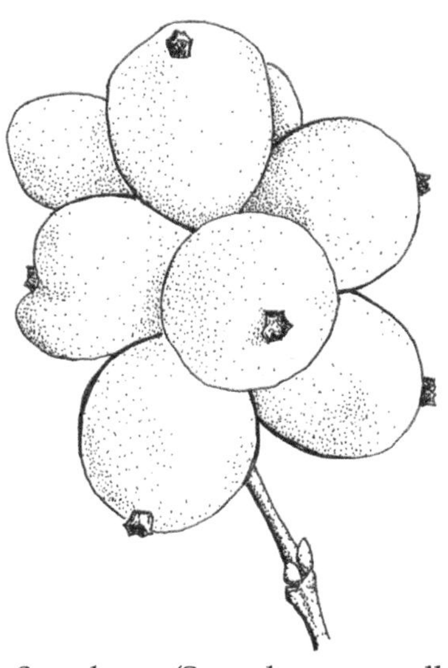

*Snowberry (*Symphocarpas alba*) keeps its white berries all winter.*

* * *

The circulating flock of little birds in our neighborhood includes both lesser and American goldfinches, pine siskins, black-capped chickadees, juncos, nuthatches, and the downy woodpeckers. It's hard to say which I enjoy more, the exquisite Townsend's warblers or the elegant varied thrush.

Those of us who feed birds in the summer need to pay attention to our feathered friends now, when the living can be tough. Feed in the wild is scarce; many birds now rely on the kindness of bird feeders. Keep seed feeders full and hummingbird feeders available by bringing them inside on freezing nights. Birds need energy to maintain life functions in temperatures below 0° C. Remember to clean outside birdseed feeders regularly, at least once a week. When they get damp, which happens even in sheltered spots, mold grows quickly. Some of the molds are toxic to birds and all of them will clog up the bird feeder port, preventing birds from getting anything. Birds appreciate a supply of fresh water, too.

Keeping the suet cages well stocked invites regular visitation of little birds. The bushtits tend to stick together in large, coherent groups. It is hilarious to watch a dozen or so trying to crowd onto one suet feeder. I think I like chickadees best because they keep up their cheery calls even in the gloomiest winter weather.

* * *

A goose rearing up in the water and flapping his wings is goose sign language for, "I'm beating my chest. This is my pond and my spouse." During breeding and nesting season male birds are aggressive and territorial. But as soon as the young are out and able to take care of themselves, most will become friendly again, moving around in groups for safety. Similarly, the flocks of warblers, bushtits, and finches coming to your feeders this time of the year will break up as nesting season approaches. You'll see the friendly flocks again this fall. It's ironic that some humans seem to be in the hostility of breeding season throughout the year. There's a lesson to be learned from the birds' friendly flocks.

* * *

With all the rain, changes in the night sky are hard to follow. Despite my regular bedtime walks, I have seen Orion fewer than five times since he first returned to the night sky. The same goes for seeing the Pleiades, which is a little distressing. I always thought a glimpse of this seven-sister cluster brings good fortune.

* * *

A January ice storm has proven that incense cedar trees are much more susceptible than Douglas-fir to the weight of ice. Incense cedar branches litter the ground. Because this cedar is adapted to warmer zones, especially in California, it has become a species with branches too weak to support snow or ice.

Storms are also hard on the heron nests in cottonwoods along the Willamette River. Only two are left in a tree that once hosted a rookery of seven or eight nests. Three of the big branches that supported nests are gone, but there are still many good nest sites available. It will be interesting to see if the herons rebuild.

* * *

In our area, global warming tends to manifest itself as droughts that desiccate our trees, causing bigger forest fires in late summer. Even in winter, however, the influence of global warming seems to cause a disruption of normal flowering time. These years our camellia bush (*Sasanqua camellia*) begains flowering in November, although it used to begin around Christmas. By Christmas, Oregon grape flowers are opening, a month early. And in January, people have reported seeing snow queen already in bloom. It usually starts in February or March!

Great blue herons nest in clusters in cottonwoods along the Willamette River.

I see the effects of global warming in such observations, although my personal evidence is largely anecdotal. My weather mantra has always been, "Typical is not normal; normal is not typical." I call this the Rule of Exceptionality. I have long thought that Oregon weather was becoming more variable, with each year more likely to have extreme events. The growing season has certainly become less predictable. As climate change becomes more and more evident across the continent, exceptionality is becoming the rule.

* * *

Oregon does not have many native earthworms. The best known is the very rare Oregon giant earthworm, found exclu-

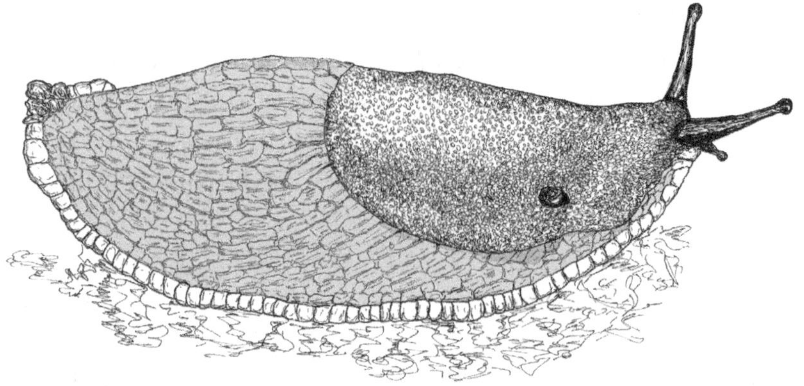

The European red slug (Arion rufus) *is one of many invasive garden pests.*

sively in the Willamette Valley and restricted to undisturbed prairie. It can be up to three feet in length.

The bugs and snails in our garden are also primarily non-native. They make up the bulk of our garden inhabitants. Many of them are pests. Sowbugs and pillbugs, for example, are frequently seen if you turn over stones or pieces of wood. They mostly eat dead plant material but can cause serious damage to seedlings.

The most obvious invasive animals in our gardens are slugs and snails. They can decimate flowers and vegetables overnight. They crowd out native fauna from urban areas; only in a natural forest are you likely to see the native banana slugs. Two of the most voracious invasives are the tiger slug and European red slug. Keeping these at bay is a challenge.

Some years won't allow it but if you have a good seed supply, be bold and start planting your garden early. Last year I planted my first row of arugula on Martin Luther King Day and it germinated within ten days. This kind of boldness works best with well drained, sandy loam in raised beds.

* * *

By the end of January the pine siskins and lesser goldfinches have left the feeders in our yard for other parts. We enjoyed their company in large flocks for most of the winter. Where did they go? That they went somewhere else tells us that winter is drawing to a close.

February

Walking down to the Delta Ponds one morning, I said goodbye to two old friends, apple trees that offered the most delicious apples to passersby. One blew down the previous February, and one was cut only this month. I'll miss seeing their blossoms. It makes me reflect that time is not measured only by hours, days, weeks or years but that it is also measured in life cycles. Life cycles may be very short or very long. None goes on forever.

* * *

In February, daylight creeps into the window earlier and earlier, lifting our moods. The natural world seems to exult as well. The initial, weak croaks of frogs will soon burst forth into a full-throated choir. The gradually warming and lengthening of days brings most of the native plants to flower. Snowdrops, wood violets, and crocuses are plentiful in town gardens. Grouse flower, goldthread, and spring beauty decorate the woodlands. The woodland floor erupts with the bright green leaves of snake root, meadowrue, nettle, and larkspur.

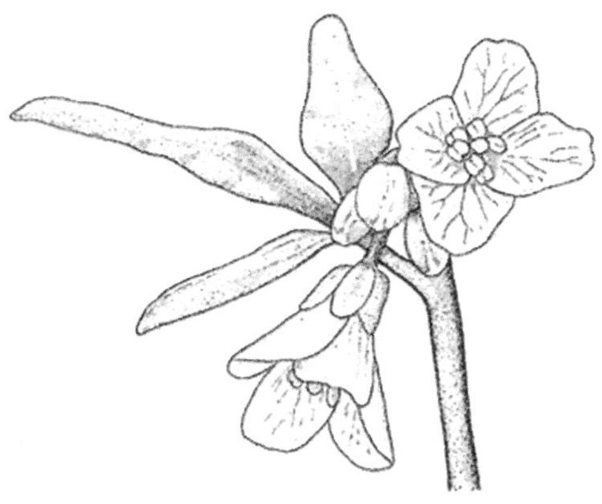

Spring beauty won its name because it is the first pink bloom of the season.

The osoberry ("Indian plum"), whose buds start swelling

Osoberry ("Indian plum") blooms early, usually by mid-February.

as early as December, bursts forth by the end of February's second week. Don't take these droopy white flowers indoors—they are pollinated by flies so they smell like old cat box litter, an odor that attracts flies.

Blooming along with the osoberry is our lovely spring beauty, so named because it is the first pink flower of the year. Changeable weather this time of year makes it hard to predict when we'll see spring beauty wildflowers, but the average first bloom in our area has historically been on February 16. This happens to be the date when Lincoln Constance was born in 1909. He was one of the most notable botanists to have grown up in Eugene and graduate from the University of Oregon. His family ritual was to search for spring beauty flowers every year on his birthday. Spring may not begin officially until the March equinox, but for Eugeneans I think it starts on Lincoln Constance's birthday.

* * *

The most common wind-pollinated trees—hazelnut, alder, and cottonwood—have begun distributing their genes in yellow dust invisible to the eye, but detectable nonetheless to the sinus membranes of the allergy prone. Cottonwoods are notable for their long season of developing catkins. Individual trees may bloom as much as six weeks earlier than others. Only the first bloomers have fat buds in February.

* * *

Gamblers begin planting their leafy crops in February. My first planting of arugula has usually sprouted by Valentine's Day, when I plant a second row of arugula and a bed of snap peas. Periodic plantings are important because arugula greens are best for a short time only. February is still too early to plant annual flowers, but you might start assembling the seed packets you'll need. Rhododendrons and azaleas will appreciate a thin spread of fresh mulch and acid fertilizer.

Warm rains bring out the worms, a welcome sight after so much weather unfavorable to worms. I like to feel that my garden is healthy when I encounter worms while turning the soil over.

* * *

Stepping outside around midnight this time of year, I notice that the Big Dipper (Ursa Major) is to the right while the big W (Cassiopeia) is to the left of the North Star. By mid-summer they will rotate, reversing their positions. Whatever their orientation, finding them means finding the North Star. And finding the North Star means finding your way.

Orion, the Hunter, is starting to disappear into the western horizon by midnight. I will miss him because there is no summer character in the sky that I know as well.

Waiting for the days to get longer, and warmer, reminds me that ancient people from northern latitudes paid more attention to the sun and the solstices. Druids and Celts built monuments like Stonehenge to mark the sun's movements. They celebrated the equinoxes and cross quarter moments. Only where the nights are clear and temperate did stargazers focus more on the moon's position in the zodiac. No wonder astrology had its roots in Babylon.

* * *

There is only one native rabbit in the Willamette Valley, the brush rabbit. It is secretive and seldom seen except by those who walk quietly in recent clearcuts or brushy areas at the edge of forests. Its breeding season begins in mid-February. Four weeks after mating, rabbits will bear their young, naked and blind, in March. Also native to Oregon is the snowshoe hare, which is technically not a rabbit. It also feeds mainly at night, but tends to live in deeper, coniferous forests. Young hares are born with hair and their eyes open.

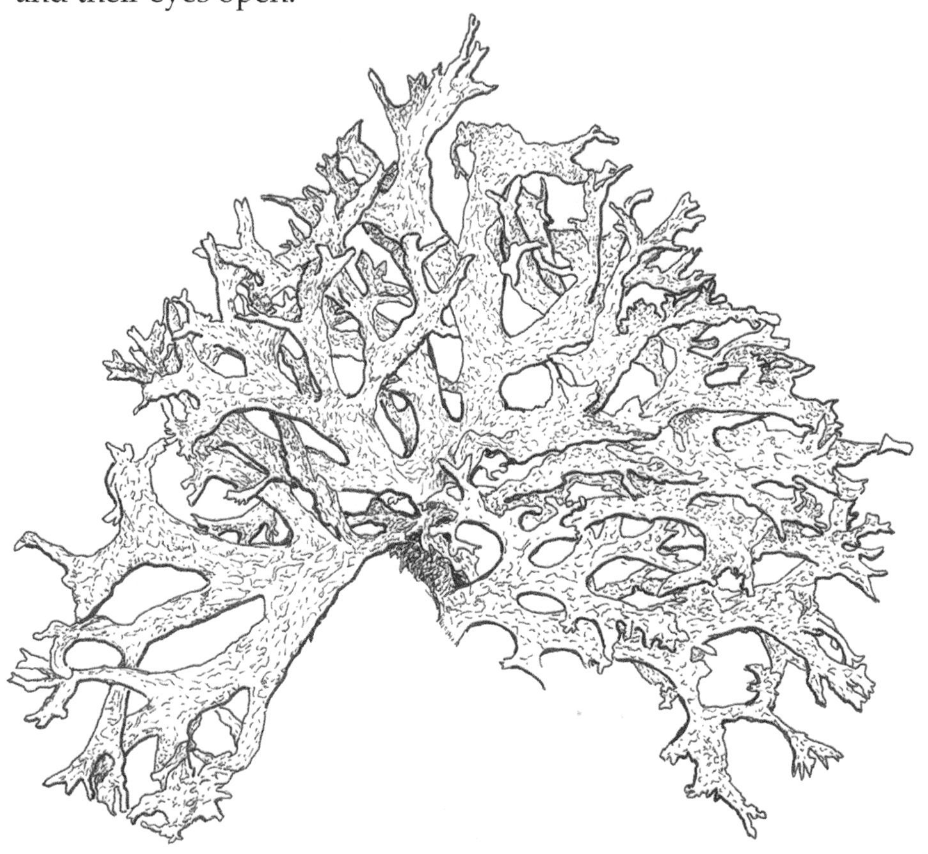

*Why does antler lichen (*Evernia prunastri*) fall from trees in winter?*

* * *

Walking down urban streets, the developing spears of moss capsules glisten orange on a sunny day. The young capsules of the largest mosses have more nutrients than any other part of the plants. They are most digestible when spores are still immature. Mice graze on them, leaving behind a miniature thicket of beheaded stalks.

Mosses that grow on tree branches are quite different from

terrestrial species. Why do these mosses fall out of trees in winter? If you look, it's easy to see the fallen clumps of gray-green lichen and dark green moss in grassy areas under the city's old bigleaf maples and oaks. For years I blamed wind storms on the rain of lichen and moss, but that never struck me as the whole story.

Recently the Mount Pisgah Arboretum caretaker remarked that Steller's jays were tearing moss clumps out of oaks, foraging for critters hidden in the moss. Aha! In my neighborhood I figure it is mostly crows and scrub jays. I have also seen crows tearing up clumps of moss on a roadside, obviously hunting for insects. Although it now seems to me that birds are responsible for the fallen moss, I'm discovering that the lichens are pulled off by fox squirrels. I wonder if these animals somehow know that the rain of young mosses, lichens, and liverworts is an important way to distribute nutrients to the soil, benefitting the old trees that support them? The short-lived species sustain the long-lived ones, and vice versa!

* * *

February brings a change in the number and kinds of birds visiting our home feeders. Many birds have moved away to look for nesting sites. Steller's jays attack suet vigorously. You can hear chickadees singing already. Installing a bird house now with a 1⅛-inch hole will attract a chickadee family while keeping out pesky house sparrows.

Steller's jays are hungry for suet in February.

Huge flocks of Canada geese cackling overhead means migrations are beginning. Down at the Delta Ponds, it is a joy to watch the northern shov-

On a sunny day in late winter, bring binoculars to the Delta Ponds to watch ring-necked ducks (left) and the American wigeon (below).

elers do their circle dances. Pairs swim around in tight circles, about a yard in diameter, seemingly forever. They're courting, pairing up for breeding in anticipation of flying north in April to nest. Early on a cold, foggy morning I saw a flock of lesser scaup keeping watch over ponds just below the Greenway Bridge. Nearby, a cormorant and a heron shared a log, their heads under their wings, waiting for the sun to come out.

Mallards have paired off in the Delta Ponds too. When the sun comes out, plan to visit the ponds for a "Duck Watching Day." Grab your binoculars and look here for gadwall, ring-necked duck, bufflehead, American coot, double-crested cormorant, American wigeon, great blue heron, and great egret. Less common but frequent in these ponds are wood duck, hooded merganser, pied-billed grebe and green heron.

Flocks of fat robins will be looking for nest sites soon. I can hardly wait for the call of the song sparrow!

March

It's simply thrilling to watch the progression of spring this time of the year. The rainy season isn't over but the woodland wildflowers are starting to bloom. The peak flush of blossoms builds after the equinox. Bigleaf maple buds burst by month's end.

A string of four or five sunny days inspires a flurry of work in the yard and garden: Fertilize the rhodies and spread fresh mulch on the perennial beds. Onion starts don't mind occasional frost, so plant them now. If you like arugula and haven't sown seeds yet, get going. Plant peas. Then pray for rain.

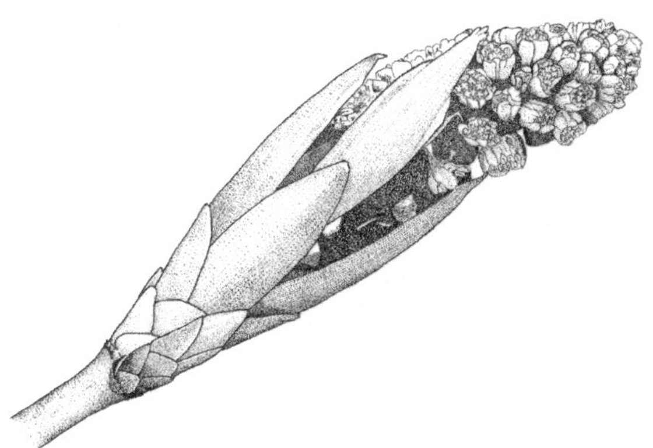

*The buds of bigleaf maple (*Acer macrophyllum*) begin to burst by the end of March.*

Quick, get seed potatoes before they sell out! Gardeners get so excited in March that the supply of seed potatoes is often gone before it's time to plant them. In temperate regions like Ireland, the traditional potato planting date is Saint Patrick's Day. In Oregon, waterlogged soil is a sign that you need to wait. If you're desperate, build a raised potato bed and cover it with a tarp. Keeping the rain off the ground may allow you to set your spuds earlier.

* * *

The same spotted towhee came to my yard so regularly that I recognized its call.

When a day dawns bright and clear, returning migrant songbirds greet the warmth of morning with tweeted arias of territorial claims. When the same towhee took up residence across the street for the second year in a row, I realized that he might have been there for many years, but that I had only learned to recognize his call the previous year.

It is good to see herons returning to the nests in the cottonwoods of east Delta Ponds. They haven't used this rookery for several years. Are there more fish in the ponds than before? A cormorant gobbling down a big fish suggests that there are. The goldeneyes are making love dances in the ponds. All the ducks and geese have paired. Soon there will be fluffy ducklings and goslings to coo over.

* * *

By the middle of March over two dozen kinds of wildflowers are in bloom. Some people may be anxious that the rate is not as fast as they would imagine a warm spring warrants. They want everything to bloom right now. The problem with this attitude is lack of appreciation of plant time. Watching a plant grow day by day, just a few minutes at a time, will help develop a sense of plant time. Focusing on the pattern will reveal change every day. The pattern is lovely every day, long before the flower buds burst open, a little different each time.

One of the great comforts of getting older is observing how the seasons return. The neighbor's daffodils are coming up as usual. Cottonwood buds are releasing their familiar, fragrant balm on warm days. Pussy willows are getting fuzzy. Towhees are searching for a nest, Bewick's wrens are warbling, and migrating robins are foraging for worms. The familiar cycle of nature gives me a surge of pleasure.

* * *

The white snowberries of January started to turn brown and shrivel last month. Now, approaching the equinox, snowberry buds are swelling to release the first greens of spring. The valley forest has a magic air in March, its understory flush with vibrant shoots. The broadleaf tree canopy still has naked branches, making the underbrush foliage seem even greener. When the sun lights up the ground it's hard not to throw off the job and walk outside. The air is sweet and the birds are singing.

I am particularly fond of vine maple because its leaves keep their fresh, green color of spring throughout the summer, especially under a forest canopy. In fall they will turn bright red, providing some of the best autumn color in our area.

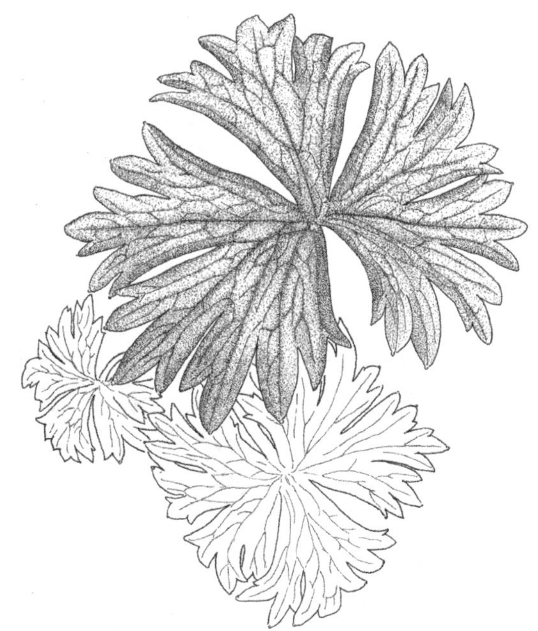

Tall larkspur's green leaves in March portend a stalk of blue flowers in May.

One of the most prominent herbaceous plants in our area this month is poison hemlock. Its huge leaves and spotted stems, often growing near urban waterways, look as luscious as carrots, but they are deadly. Poison hemlock was Socrates' choice for a suicide potion. Even using a hollow stem as a straw can be fatal. It is especially abundant in the valley between Medford and Ashland. It looks very much like parsley. If it didn't smell so bad there probably would be many more deaths reported.

If you are foraging for wild greens, stick to safe ones like stinging nettle, unmistakable with its stinging hairs. If you cook nettles the sting will vanish. The result is a healthy vegetable resembling spinach. Harvest them soon, or they will get tough and stringy. How stringy? Nettle fibers were used for rope by the coastal zone's First Peoples.

* * *

At the Delta Ponds, beavers have completely girdled a big ash tree. It is a solitary individual that sheltered gracefully on a small island, but now it is doomed. I wonder how long it will take for

Beavers have been gnawing on the ash trees by the Delta Ponds.

the dead tree to fall? It still has a lot of wood left in its trunk. If it doesn't fall soon, the beaver's gnawing will have been wasted because the tasty bark of the branches will be too dry to eat.

* * *

Mosses look luxuriant now, especially if a mild winter has encouraged robust growth. The maturing capsules of the capillary thread moss ("nodding bobbers") are nodding and bobbing prominently on concrete blocks and walls everywhere.

Frogs, newts and salamanders are laying eggs in ponds. Tadpoles and larvae should be observed in ponds and still backwaters by the end of the month. It is important for them to begin early, to avoid being stranded in drying puddles.

Birds will not begin nesting until their home tree has leaves. It is particularly dramatic to watch herons return to their nests. By the end of the month, they will be sitting on eggs or feeding their young.

The winter steelhead run is almost over. The spring run of Chinook salmon begins next month.

Gray whale cows and their calves are migrating north in good numbers this month. Perhaps the most fabulous place to watch whales is the old stone lookout shelter on Cape Perpetua, at the top of the Saint Perpetua Trail. From there you can see far over the ocean, protected from wind and rain. The hike is very steep but a road allows one to drive up most of the way. Go early in the day, as the parking lot at the top is small.

* * *

At least two dozen different kinds of flowers should now be blooming at the Mount Pisgah Arboretum. The western buttercup is the gay yellow of the open hillsides while the soft yellows in the woods are from the fawn lilies. Delicate pinks

Hike Mount Pisgah to see slopes full of yellow western buttercups.

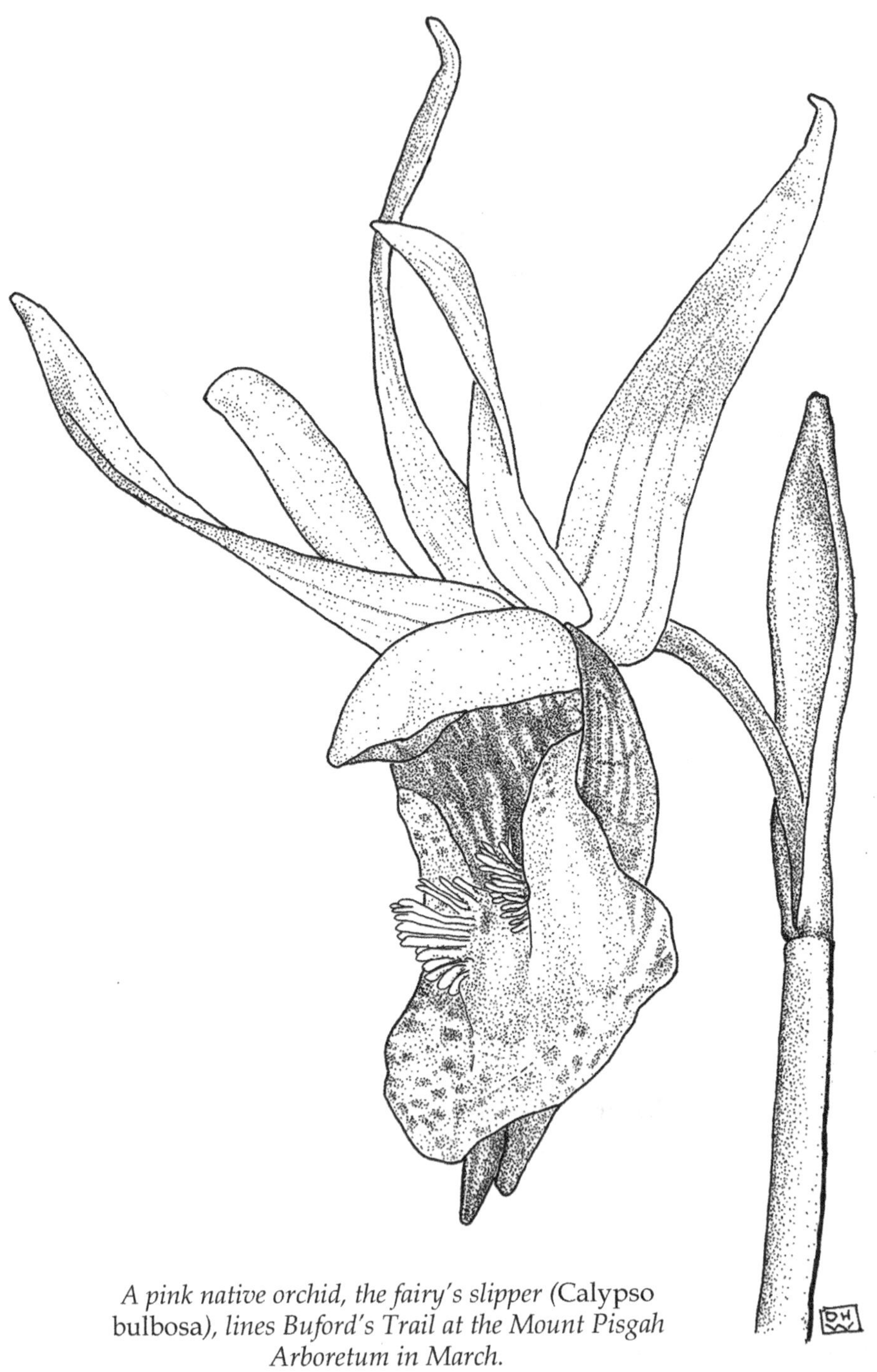

A pink native orchid, the fairy's slipper (Calypso bulbosa)*, lines Buford's Trail at the Mount Pisgah Arboretum in March.*

come from the calypso orchids, which line Buford's Trail. This is my favorite time of the year to hike up Mount Pisgah itself, before the vibrant greens of spring give way to the sepias of summer.

The spring waves of wildflower blooms remind me of waves crashing on the beach, but in very slow motion. This is what makes time-lapse movies of flowers opening so appealing. When time is speeded up it is easier to appreciate the slow but steady dance of a flower blossoming.

* * *

Almost thirty years ago a new, annual species of geranium showed up at the Mount Pisgah Arboretum wildflower show. It is known as shining geranium or Geranium lucidum. It spread rapidly through the woodlands of Mount Pisgah. Within ten years it became the dominant understory herb. It is now almost everywhere in western Oregon.

Considerable effort is devoted to combatting species that disrupt native ecosystems. English ivy was originally widely planted, but now it is illegal to plant because it has proven to be fiercely invasive. With the shining geranium, however, there was never a chance to keep it at bay. It spread so rapidly that we now have to accept it as being here to stay.

The shining geranium is an invasive that has spread rapidly in woodlands.

Many weedy species came with the arrival of Europeans in North America. To the original natives of the continent, Europeans brought with them an invasive culture and invasive plant species. We prefer to call the human invaders settlers, pioneers, or migrants, so why not the plants? Their arrival was not by choice but they migrated thanks to opportunities given by some agent like wind or animals. Successful spread is what makes them "invasive."

We cannot always determine if a new arrival is a natural,

opportunistic migrant or a human-mediated invasive. But when something like shining geranium arrives, it doesn't matter whether you call it a recent migrant or an invasive. Its presence must be simply accepted. It seems to me that those who are now called "illegal immigrants" deserve similar acceptance.

* * *

For the past six months or so, some animal has been digging holes next to the path along the ponds on the east side of Delta Highway. Tracks left in mud on the path after a winter rain finally gave us a clue: nutria. Their distinctive tracks include a tail streak between foot prints. Nutria like to dig up roots, worms, and bugs. They seemed to have been eating lots of the roots of poison hemlock, now that its leaves have sprouted. Considering how deadly this plant is to humans, I wondered how nutria could survive such a meal. Then I met the volunteers who work with the city habit restoration program and found they have been rooting out poison hemlock for the past month. Nutria are off the hook.

Robins really do listen for earthworms.

* * *

The European nightcrawler is one of our most abundant non-native garden invasives, but unlike most exotic species it stands out as having a positive impact in our gardens. If you want to see them without digging wait for a good, warm, night rain to drive them out of the ground to breathe. They litter the streets the next morning, trapped by curbs. On such mornings, robins are delighted.

We no longer have many native earthworms in the Pacific Northwest. Pleistocene glaciation of lowland soils, especially in Washington and British Columbia, is believed to be one reason our native earthworm inventory has declined to fewer than a half dozen species.

Charles Darwin is the godfather of earthworm appreciation. His final book, The Formation of Vegetable Mould Through the Action of Worms, was published in 1882, the year before his death. He had been studying earthworms for more than 40 years. He estimated that English farmland had an average of 53,767 earthworms per acre recycling the soil. As in all his evolutionary works, he showed how earthworm's slow, nearly imperceptible changes develop dramatic effects over long periods of time. He even observed how stone monoliths, such as at Stonehenge, are gradually being buried by earthworm activity.

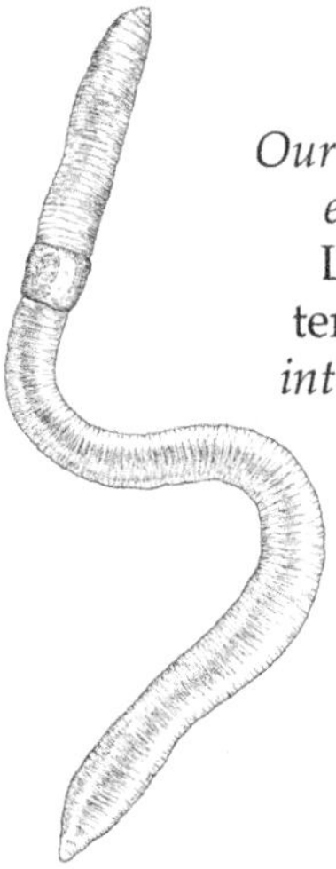

Our most common earthworm, Lumbricus terrestris, *was introduced from Europe.*

Perhaps earthworm migration has changed our landscape almost as dramatically as human migration.

* * *

One of the rituals of my morning cup of coffee is checking where the rising sun casts its rays across the living room. At winter solstice, the light shines in my eyes through the window in the southeast corner. Little by little, the sun rises farther north on the horizon. Each day, the sunbeams land more and more to my right. After a few weeks, the sun no longer shines in my eyes through that window. Not until the sun shines through the next window north am I blinded again. Our living room windows act as a kind of seasonal sundial.

By summer solstice, the rising sun shines in my eyes through a north window. That is, if I get up early enough. Sunrise time shifts from 7:43 a.m. at winter solstice to 5:30 in the morning at summer solstice (it would be 4:30 a.m. if we stuck to standard time). The daily change is gradual but the rate of change is not constant. Sunrise time changes rapidly during the period around each equinox but slows down around the solstices.

The daily change in sunrise approaching spring equinox is something we feel in our bones. Nature feels it, too, as the romantic activities of breeding birds get insistent. The expanding leaves of perennial herbs are practically jumping out of the ground. Buds are bursting on trees and shrubs. The number of wildflowers blooming just keeps increasing.

The "pussy willow" buds of Salix sitchensis *burst open by the end of March.*

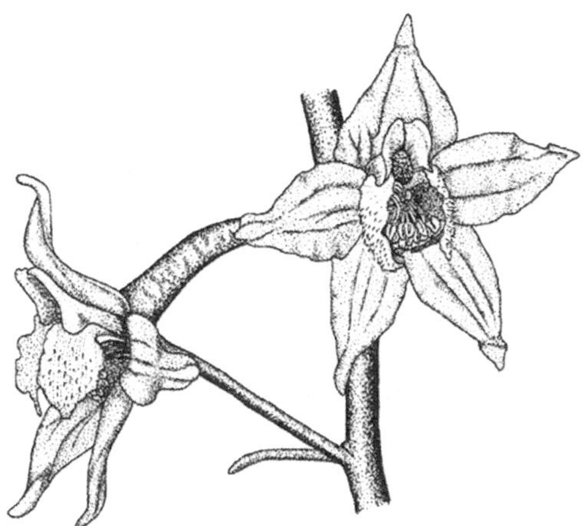

Tall larkspur jumps up and blooms in April.

April

"March-April" is the busiest month of the year from a plant's point of view. Day length is changing fast, getting longer and longer on the summer side of the equinox. Bursts of sun and plenty of rain pumps rapid growth. All the energy stored in roots, rhizomes, and bulbs is emerging every day in an intense, slow dance of sun worship.

Woodland herbs move fast now, keeping just ahead of the trees above them. Once the trees' leafy canopy fills in, little light is left for the woodland floor dwellers. The tall larkspur, bleeding heart, fringe cup, and maianthemum lilies (false solomon's seal), that have been pushing up slowly for the past few months, now unfurl and jump up to offer flowers to foraging insects.

The Papilio zeliacon *caterpillar.*

Newly hatched caterpillars of butterflies are eating fresh leaves. On up the food chain, nesting song birds swoop in to eat the insects that are taking advantage of the plants taking advantage of the sun. Hawks swoop in to hunt the song birds, joining the feast of spring.

* * *

Sunny day excitement makes it hard not to get ahead of your garden sense, planting things too soon. This month you'll see more and more vegetable starts for sale in racks outside the local markets. Hold off on buying those tomatoes and peppers. It really is too early to plant much besides peas, onions, broccoli, carrots, radishes, and beets. The frost-free season traditionally begins somewhere around the middle of April, and it will take another six weeks for soil to warm up enough for optimal growth of corn or beans.

If you're eager to get busy in your garden, clean up the beds to stay ahead of the weeds. I just turn around and the flowerbed I weeded last week needs weeding again. The little bittercress annuals sprouting in your garden are *Cardamine,* which I say rhymes with *goddaminny.* These tiny plants need only a few warm days to germinate, put up their flowers and go to seed. I try to pull them before the seedpods mature. Their mature seedpods explode on touch, flinging tiny seeds in all directions. That is a guarantee that you will be weeding yet again.

The bulb of blue camas (Camassia quamash) *was an important food for native tribes.*

* * *

What is it about the call of a chickadee on a sunny morning that makes

What is it about the call of the black-capped chickadee?

the heart sing? Love is in the air! How wonderful it is that these birds reside in town with us. I can't imagine having to live in a city neighborhood without chickadees and robins. It is good to pause and give thanks for winged joy.

With the equinox behind us, rapidly lengthening days have us roaring headlong towards summer. The main flowering season crowds into the next two months, before the long dry period that characterizes our late summer. It's time to dust off those field guides and polish the hand lenses.

Camas will be blooming by the end of the month. We have two kinds in this area, the giant camas of upland seepy slopes and the small camas of wetlands with standing water in winter. Camas was an important food source for the original inhabitants of the area. Roasted in pit ovens, it is sweet and nourishing. Boiled, however, it has the consistency of library paste.

* * *

"The force that through the green fuse drives the flower ..." April could well be Dylan Thomas month. Looking up at trees, I am overwhelmed by the urgency of the leaves unfurling and flowers bursting from every bud. Walking under cottonwoods along the riverbank paths makes me giddy with the fragrance released by their fallen resinous buds. All six local native willows have their buds popping open. Pussy willows earn their name, with young catkins as softly furry as a kitten. The technical term "catkin" comes from Dutch for little cat!

Incense cedar pollen dispersal took place back in January. Heaps of spent pollen cones that accumulated in rain gutters gave evidence of the millions of pollen grains that blew over the landscape. In April there may be another rain of cones, this time the aborted female cones that didn't get enough seeds fertilized to make it worth investing in full development of seed cones. It demonstrates that wind pollination, despite seeming to exhibit overproduction of pollen, is not always effective. Darn that winter rain!

The larger animals had their breeding season last fall and are now in late gestation, getting ready to bring forth young when nature's bounty is most abundant. Birds and small mammals are entering their main breeding season.

The sex life of flowering plants is not nearly as obvious. The bigleaf maple has one of the most complex. It has two different forms of unisexual flowers, complementary pairs that emerge at different times on two mating types.

* * *

April is the month we'll be saying goodbye to most of the wintering waterfowl. I am going to miss the buffleheads. The resident early birds have already started nesting while many migrants are just arriving. They will be checking to see if the old nest is suitable for refurbishing for another season. If it is, they will soon start singing songs of domestic joy. The bushtit flocks don't break up while nesting and feeding young. They do forage by themselves now, unaccompanied by their usual winter companions, juncos and chickadees.

* * *

This month bumblebee queens emerge and begin foraging. Unlike honeybees, bumblebee colonies begin from a single, fertilized, hibernating female. This queen must find a nest and begin a new colony. She will start by laying eggs and feeding workers. When there are enough workers, she will stay in the nest and be fed by them while she produces drones and females at the end of the season. The mated females will hibernate to emerge as queens next spring.

* * *

For the next couple of weeks the windshield of my pickup will be dusted with the yellow powder of pollen. Cone-bearing trees use the "success in numbers" method of pollen dispersal. Their tiny, dry pollen grains weigh practically nothing. Tossed on whirling winds like ping pong balls in the ocean, it is only against formidable odds that a pollen grain gets blown into the protective bracts of the seed cones to perform the dance of birds and bees.

Without either birds or bees, wind-pollinated trees stick to the old reliable strategy: Make enough pollen grains to fill the air. After their pollen is dispersed, Douglas-fir trees drop pollen cones by the millions. Living under a Douglas-fir canopy, I have to scoop them out of my gutters by the bucket load. Studied under a hand lens, they look like tiny golden-brown lilies.

Douglas-fir trees drop pollen cones by the millions in April.

* * *

The ferns you see growing on mossy tree branches are licorice ferns. Like moss, they time their spore capsules to mature in April. Two months from now, after the spores have dispersed, the leaves of the licorice ferns will curl up and fall to the ground. Meanwhile, the terrestrial ferns are just starting to uncurl new fronds. The sword fern is unusual in that its fronds do not uncurl from a spiral fiddlehead like most ferns but instead have a drooping hook that looks like an elephant's trunk.

At this time of year mosses luxuriate, so my eye is drawn to mosses on seepy rock walls. On just one walk I found a hillside with at least twenty different kinds of mosses!

* * *

Do birds return to the same nest year after year? All winter, when the deciduous trees are bare, I look at clots of debris high in their branches and try to pick out which are just clumps of leaves and which are nests. The obstacle to solving this puzzle is that the old nests are obscured by leaves by the time birds come back. It's hard to tell if the nests are used again.

Only occasional observations have presented themselves over

Great blue herons like to hunker down when they're not actively fishing.

the past years of bird watching. Chickadees nested in one of our nest boxes two years in a row. A spotted towhee has nested in the hedge across the street for five or more years.

Because the herons at East Delta Pond start their nesting season long before the cottonwoods leaf out, it's easier to keep track of reused nests. Why do our local great blue herons nest in late leafing trees? They seem exposed to predation much longer than if they used early leafing trees. In fact, a rookery broke up several years ago when a pair of bald eagles started marauding the young. The number of active nests plummeted, probably fledging no young at all in some years. Lately there has been a resurgence, with six nests in use. Four are old ones, while two are new or dramatically refurbished.

Warm, sunny days bring out everybody to stretch their wings. Literally in the case of birds, figuratively in the case of quiescent snakes and dozing turtles. And, of course, me too!

Showy milkweed hosts Monarch butterflies, and an occasional fly.

May

Hooray for May, when wildflower blooming reaches its peak in the Willamette Valley! The annual wildflower show at the Mount Pisgah Arboretum in Buford Park celebrates this flush on the Sunday after Mother's Day. Monkeyflowers from the mountains, prairie stars from the grasslands, and products of local native plant nurseries are on display.

On your drive to the wildflower show, watch for camas blooming in low grassy areas along the freeway. Blue camas, at its peak early in May, was a food staple for indigenous people. The rarer ivory-colored camas grows along the freeway from Sutherlin to Riddle. Its color is different from the pure white of albino forms of the related blue species.

* * *

Now it is finally time to plant vegetables out in the garden. You want their roots to be well established for productive growth when the weather warms up in July and August. I have come to appreciate knee pads when working in the garden. Knee pads have brought me closer to the little plants I dance with all the time. I have become fond of the red henbit, the prettiest of the humble flowering plants we call weeds.

Mowing and weeding, I love the smell of plants cut and torn off. I wonder if I am an instinctive gatherer, rather than hunter, with a sap lust instead of blood lust? Slugs are afoot these days, eating their way through the lilies and primroses. If you want to pick one up to toss away, you had better use a leaf or other wrap because they produce an alarm slime when disturbed. It is amazingly sticky and won't wash off with soap and water.

* * *

The Oregon white oak (known as Garry oak outside of Oregon) is the last of our native trees to leaf out. The oaks are genetically predisposed to avoid late season snow damage by waiting until

California black oak (left) grows from Lane County south into California. Oregon white oak (or Garry oak, at right), grows from California to Canada.

May to get a full crown of leaves. Bud-burst, with pollen catkins suspended to shake in the wind, begins at the end of April. The female flowers, like those of most wind-pollinated trees, are all but invisible to any except oak lovers. Only the development of acorns later in the season shows their location.

Getting out into the oak woods means watching out for poison oak. Its leaves are just unfurling so they are barely noticeable, but they are as virulent now as any time of the year. An alert is also needed for those allergic to grass pollen. The count starts to climb toward the end of this month, peaking in June.

The wild cucumber is growing fast, extending grasping tendrils upwards. All the early flowers are male. These are the ones on stalks. The female flowers appear later, singly in the angle between leaf stalk and stem.

Out in the woods the deer and elk are dropping fawns. Remember to leave a fawn alone if you encounter one hunkered down in a mountain meadow. It is not abandoned, just waiting for mommy to return from her foraging. Seal pups on the beach are similarly just fine, waiting for return of their nursing mother.

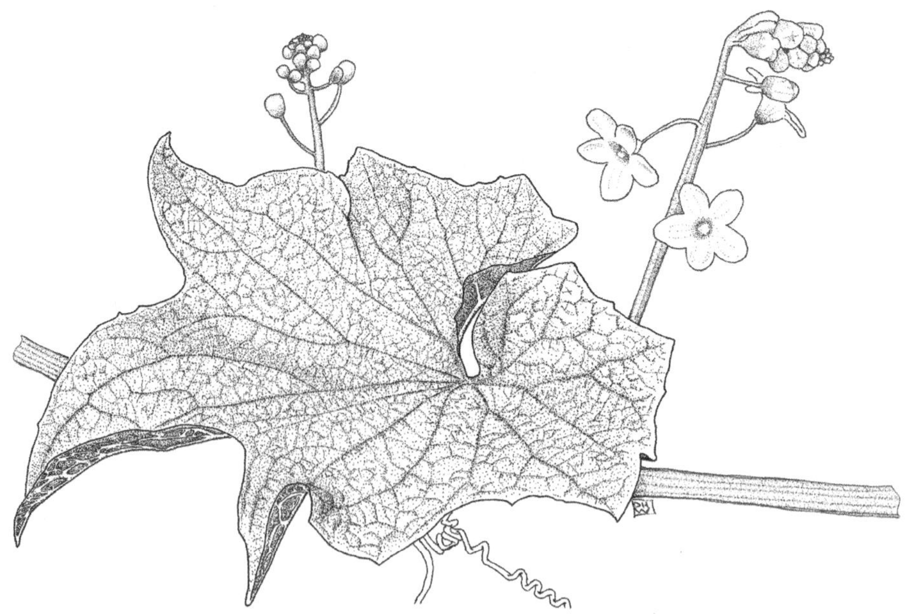

The white male flowers of wild cucumber bloom first.

They may look stranded but should not be disturbed. A too-close presence will keep the mothers away.

* * *

The geese that crouched over their nests last month have abandoned their vigil. At first I feared that their nests had been raided by predators, the eggs destroyed. Happily, I was wrong. Two new goose families are now bobbing around the Delta Ponds, one family with six goslings and one with seven. It is such a pleasure to watch these fuzzy little bundles of cuteness through binoculars. Seeing them swim around, tended by their watchful parents, makes me think that Mother's Day in May is a natural celebration of all nature.

The temptation to feed goslings is great, but don't give in! Feeding bread to ducks or geese makes their bones grow too fast, out of sync with their feathers. The resulting warped wing tips, known as "angel wing," is a permanent disability that prevents them from flying.

On a sunny day the Delta Ponds are also a great place for turtle watching. They line up on anchored logs in early morning.

Slider turtles collect ultraviolet rays with their shells, so they love to sun.

The leaves of the cottonwood trees are now all expanded. The crown is full and gradually changing shades from a bright spring green to a tough, dark summer green. Inside the leaf buds—but not the flower buds—is a resin that smells very sweet. It is the American source of Balm of Gilead.

* * *

While the herbs and shrubs are busy making seeds, the birds are also generating offspring. Hummingbirds have already fledged a nestful of hummers. Baby crows are out and about in May, crying for attention and feeding. They stay in the nest only fifteen days after hatching. That's the period of time the mommy and daddy crows are likely to attack people who come too close.

Towhees are good neighborhood friends. Their buzzy tweet lets you know they are around, that they have a nest somewhere close, even if they are not easy to see. There are three nesting pairs in our neighborhood. Each pair maintains a fairly small territory that is easy to recognize because each pair is characterized by a slightly different tone to their "tzzzeet!"

I believe there is no bird call more joyous than a robin at sunrise. Enthusiastic males declare to any lady robin in hearing distance that he offers the best territory. Once eggs are laid, it is the crowing of fatherhood.

Flowers are blooming, bugs are out: Nesting season has begun. Nesting works well now because the food source is emerging. Feeding nestlings is easy as over-wintering insect eggs hatch and turn loose hungry larvae on tender greens breaking out from winter buds.

* * *

May is the best money-making season for plant nurseries. Although new varieties of flowers are tantalizing, consider buying native species to attract native birds and butterflies. My favorites are blood currant, red elderberry, and penstemon. Fringecup (*Tellima grandiflora*) is a hugely underappreciated native that I have been known to declare Flower of the Year. Its flowers are modest, but it is easy to grow in shady spots and its leaves remain lush green throughout the summer. It makes a good companion to sword ferns, another native that does not wither in summer. Fringecup is unusual because its seeds do not germinate when their capsules open. They have a heat requirement and wait for the rainy season before sprouting.

A keen observer of the flowers along mountain stream trails

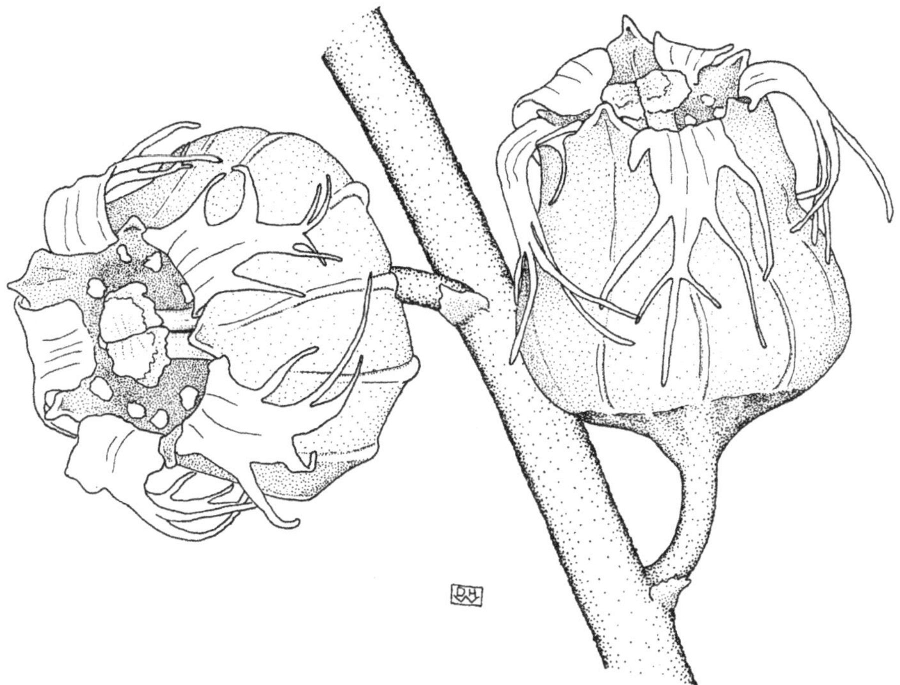

Fringecup is often overlooked, but its flower is quite delicate up close.

keeps an eye out for spots where fringecup and piggy-back plants grow together. A rare treat is finding their hybrid. These beautiful, nameless hybrids do not last long in nature. They cannot make fertile seeds.

Sword ferns and fringecups can also be collected from National Forests, if you stop at a ranger station to pick up a free permit. Both transplant well. Not all native plants do. In May the forest floor is now reaching peak flowering of the fairy slipper orchid, *Calypso bulbosa*. It is very beautiful, but it is difficult to grow and dies if transplanted.

* * *

When asked what is my favorite color, my answer is "spring green." By this I refer to the bright green of unfurling leaves on trees and shrubs. The leaves on most woody plants will darken as the season progresses but vine maples that grow in the understory have leaves that stay bright green through the season. The leaves of vine maples that grow in the open, as in the lava fields near the mountain passes, do get a darker green but then these are also the ones that turn the brightest red in fall.

* * *

May is an energizing month for western Oregon nature lovers: lots of action every day as we ride the "slow train" through solstice in June. It's a "slow train" because long days have settled in. Day length changes little until late August. There's lots of action, however, because conditions change fast. Warm days, cold days; rainy days and sunny days; sudden thundershowers follow balmy breezes drifting in from the coast.

More different wildflowers bloom on any day in May than any other month of the year. Wild animals are birthing and teaching their pups and fawns what to eat. Mountain birds have moved upslope. Migratory waterfowl head back north. Resident nesting birds are ensconced in nest boxes, hanging baskets woven from mosses, and rookeries high in riverbank cottonwoods.

The birds we enjoy watching at home feeders have temporarily disappeared. Every pair is building their nest and feeding their

Bushtits flock to a cage of suet.

young. They won't come out of watchful privacy until nestlings have fledged. They will return soon. Keep a good stock of bird seed on hand, anticipating when the feeders again will be drained as fast as in winter. Suet cages will get special attention because birds need to fatten up for migration day.

To see birds now, take a folding chair, water bottle, sketch book, and binoculars for a rejuvenating sit by the river. Learn the difference between diving ducks and dabbling ducks. One never need feel lonely. Nature entertains, comforts, and sustains us.

* * *

This is an excellent time to wander in the woods, walking favorite trails slowly and quietly, paying attention to every moss and flower. One of the natural history mentors of my youth was fond of saying, "Never go the same way twice." I took him seriously while in high school. I sought out different stream valleys to explore and hills to visit every weekend. Only in my later years did I recognize that this advice is something of a koan—a Zen paradox. Because of time, nothing stays the same. It is impossible to go the same way twice. There is always something new to see, discoveries to be made in the most familiar of places.

The Japanese practice of shinrin-yoku, forest bathing, has become popular in America as a form of nature therapy. Its beneficial effects on human physiology have been clearly demonstrated. It is often done as a group activity.

Related to shinrin yoku is seeking Waldeinsamkeit. This practice originated in the time of Mozart and Goethe, an element of German Romanticism of the late 18th century. Sometimes translated as "forest loneliness," it is better called "forest solitude." Similar to shinrin yoku, Waldeinsamkeit enriches one's spiritual wellbeing.

* * *

When I step outside at bedtime and see the Big Dipper practically overhead, I know that summer is on its way.

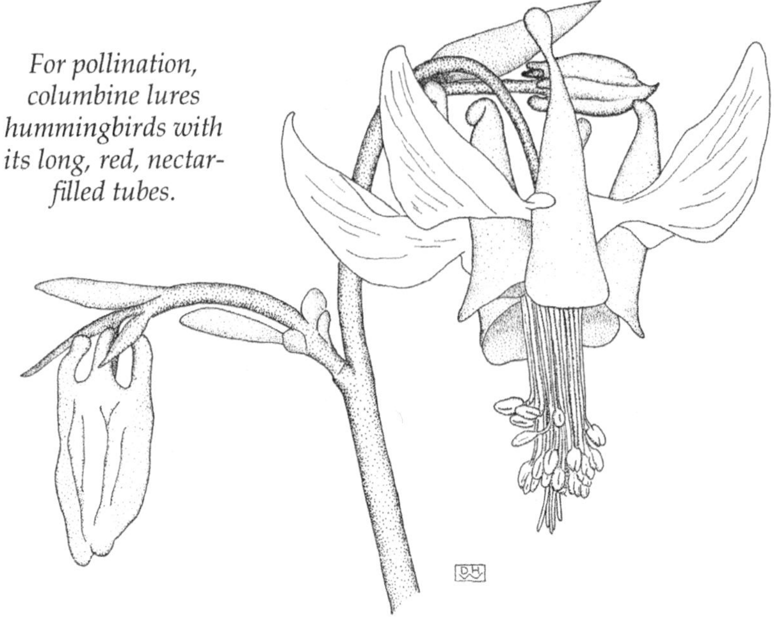

For pollination, columbine lures hummingbirds with its long, red, nectar-filled tubes.

June

June means "Solstice!" to people who track the seasons. We celebrate the longest day of the year, usually on the 20th or 21st, as the beginning of summer. Did you ever wonder why the solstice didn't mark the middle of summer? The hottest days of the year always come after June because it takes a long time for the oceans to warm up. Ocean temperature controls the temperature of air that blows inland.

Licorice ferns have dried up on the tree trunks that serve as their home. Like the mosses they grow with, they flourish in the rainy season and go dormant in the summer. Their spores probably won't germinate until fall, but nobody knows for sure.

* * *

A wave of wildflower bloom moves up the mountains in June, each meadow having a later peak of flowering the higher up you go. It is interesting to follow the species that grow at all elevations, like bleeding heart and columbine. Last month they bloomed on the valley floor. Come July, they will open up on Cascade ridge tops. Hummingbirds follow columbines up the hill. These graceful flowers, with deep nectar pockets and showy red colors, are adapted to be pollinated by the long beaks of hummingbirds. Who pollinates the bleeding heart is a mystery, but who eats them is well known. Caterpillars of the Parnassian butterfly feed exclusively on bleeding heart.

* * *

Mother's Day is close to May Day, a traditional time for fertility festivals. The June solstice is near Father's Day, a time to emphasize nurturing and maturing. Gardeners should have all the big plants in the ground – tomatoes, squash, peppers, and eggplant. Remember that if you want these plants to feed you, first you must feed them. A little fertilizer is a low-risk growth investment.

Rufous hummingbird.

* * *

When June is rainy you can expect more slugs and snails in the garden. If you don't want to use commercial slug bait, you can lure them into a covered pie tin with a little beer, where they drown. Like the pill bugs and earthworms, garden slugs and snails are not native. Almost all the urban pests are exotic, even most squirrels. The eastern fox squirrel has displaced our native gray squirrel in all parts of town except the heavily wooded parks.

Gardeners know that even though Oregon is thought of as a rainy state, long dry spells are likely in the next months. If you invest in a timer that sends daily water to your petunias and potatoes you'll be able to take long hikes in the mountains without worry. Remember, snakes and lizards are your garden friends. They eat what you might otherwise poison: slugs and bugs.

* * *

This is the greenest time of year. All the trees and shrubs have expanded their leaves. The leaves have not yet fully toughened up so most of them retain the bright, spring green that's my favorite color. Still, the lowlands are drying out. The licorice ferns have turned yellow-brown and are falling off the tree branches. Only the ground dwelling colonies in damp, shady spots are keeping their green for a few more weeks.

We notice that very few birds are coming to the feeders. Migrations are over and the nesting season is in full swing. Birds are protecting their territories so they don't gather at feeders. We will see them again with their fledglings.

The biggest surprise for me is the chickadee family using an old decorative nest box which was gifted to me many years ago. Corn cobs, millet heads and lichens were glued to make it attractive to birds but they hardly ever came to feed off it. Just as I was about to take it down because it was falling apart, chickadees started exploring it and now are feeding young. Unlike other nestlings I've known, these are very quiet to avoid bringing attention to themselves.

The samaras (winged seed carriers) of bigleaf maple grow in pairs, but fly away singly like helicopters.

* * *

June is a big gardening month.

Early winter greens have been used up and cleared away while the sugar snap peas should reach maximum production. The solstice marks when the bush beans should have been planted. I like both peas and beans because they are so easy to grow from seed. The critical issue is protecting the seedlings from sneaky herbivores like pill bugs and sow bugs. These nonnative pests hide in mulch or between rocks of the raised beds. They creep out at night to devour the tender plumule just as it starts to emerge from between the cotyledons. If that tiny bit of leaf bud is lost, the whole plant is doomed.

Farmers markets are flush with vegetable garden starts. Our traditional vegetable season starts late because of our typical cool spring but lasts long into the fall. I harvest hot peppers in October. I encourage supporting the local organic farmers by buying well-rooted starts. For a small garden, it seems to make more sense than investing in starting from seed indoors. Only my peas and beans are seeded directly into the ground, one following the other.

I tried an experiment by planting garlic last October. They are now robust plants with more growth expected before a midsummer harvest. The snap peas I planted in February are over six feet tall. All will be harvested by the end of June. After they are gone, climbing string beans will replace them on the trellis. I wish I had more space for zucchini and cucumbers.

* * *

This is a banner month for the bigleaf maple, when its winged fruits, called double samaras, are being produced in great abundance. I have been following their development on a neighborhood tree, taking pictures of one particular flower cluster every week or ten days. I thought this was an ordinary tree but only recently noticed that instead of the usual pair of wings, more than half the flowers have triple samaras and a few with four wings are seen. It demonstrates that trees, like people, have individuality.

* * *

Snow still blocks trails in the high country. Long days are

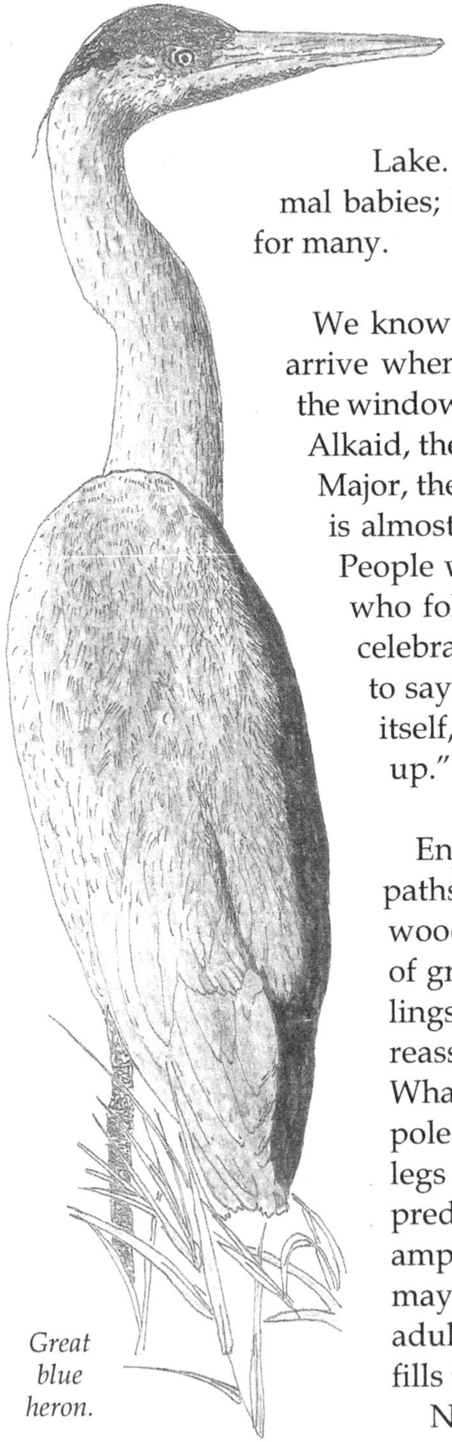

ideal for low-elevation exploration. Stream fishing should be good while fishing is picking up at Diamond Lake. Watch for fawns and other animal babies; birthing season is in full swing for many.

* * *

We know the summer solstice is soon to arrive when the rising sun shines through the windows on the north side of the house. Alkaid, the star at the tip of the tail of Ursa Major, the end of the Big Dipper's handle, is almost directly overhead at midnight. People who follow the stars and people who follow the sun are prepared for a celebration. As an old friend was wont to say, "Logic today must take care of itself, the sun's in the hills living it up."

* * *

Enjoy walking on the riverbank paths. Standing under tall cottonwood trees listening to the murmur of great blue herons tending to nestlings in the rookery above is deeply reassuring. Play in ponds for fun. What's more fun than catching tadpoles for children to see how the legs develop? Bullfrogs, although predatory invasives, make great examples of metamorphosis. Tadpoles may take two years to develop into adults, so a big four-legged pollywog fills the hand of a two-year-old child.

Nesting season is coming to a close

Great blue heron.

this month, easily noticed with geese and turkey nestlings that leave their nests and swim or run right after hatching. One of the enjoyable sights of early summer is watching a troop of goslings or chicks paddling or scurrying around after their parents. They are out feeding for themselves, learning how to find and handle their food by following their parents. Most songbird babies stay in the nest until they are ready to fly. After they fledge and leave the nest, they are pretty much on their own.

* * *

The spring flush of flowers has reached its climax in the valley bottoms. Seedpods are developing in all but wetland plants, where flowering and fruiting tends to occur later. The dry seeds of fringecup are interesting in that they will not germinate in the summer. The seeds have a summer dormancy that prevents them from germinating during occasional rain showers. Otherwise they would dry up and die when the usual summer dry period resumes. Only after midwinter are their seeds ready to sprout.

Most flowers are relatively passive when it comes to courting a pollinator. Bright colors and sweet scents work quite well when bees and butterflies are around. Scotch broom is different in that it acts like a trap for heavy insects like bumble bees. Its stamens are spring-loaded and snap out when the petals are pushed down, slapping a load of pollen on the back of the bee.

Summer solstice is arguably the most significant of all solar events. That the sun shone straight down a well in Syrene, Egypt, every summer solstice day gave Eratosthenes the insight for determining the Earth's circumference 2,200 years ago. Stone monuments worldwide are aligned to commemorate this longest day of the year. The bronze sighting monument on the summit of Mount Pisgah has slots that line up with sunrise and sunset on the solstice. Winter solstice uses the same sighting slots as summer, but reversed.

* * *

Gardens need to be taken seriously now, as the main growing season is ahead of us.

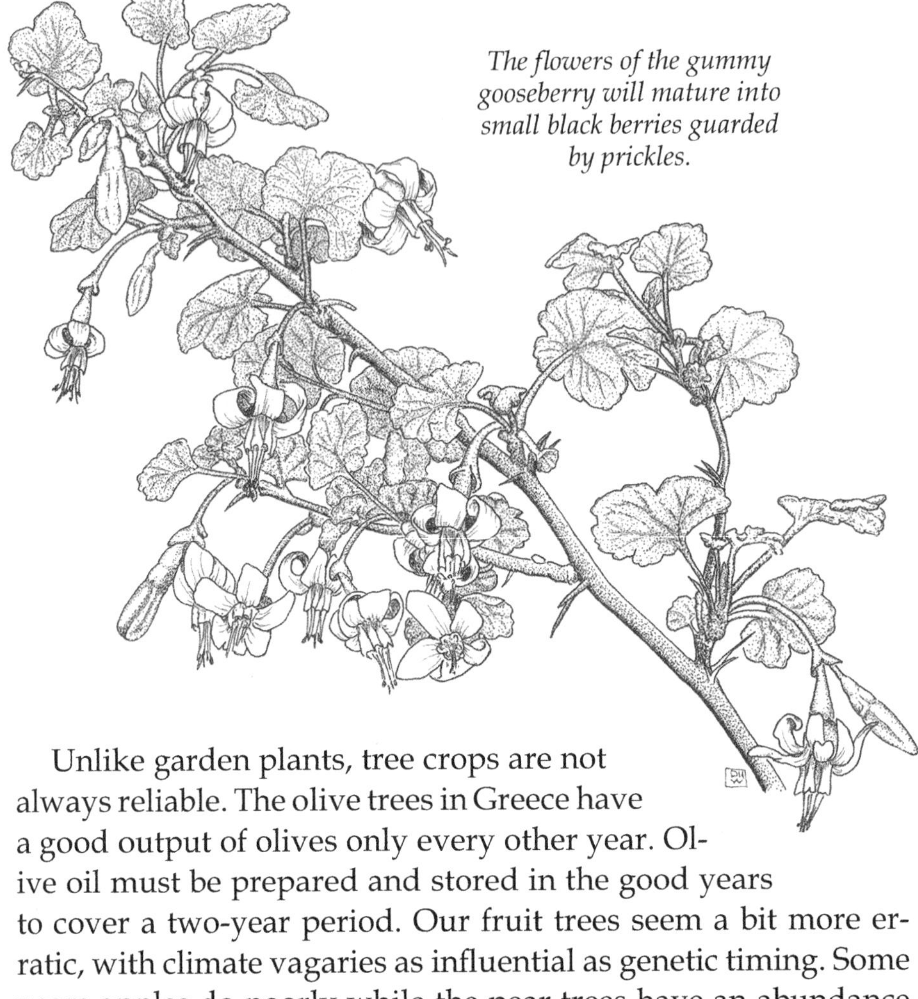
The flowers of the gummy gooseberry will mature into small black berries guarded by prickles.

Unlike garden plants, tree crops are not always reliable. The olive trees in Greece have a good output of olives only every other year. Olive oil must be prepared and stored in the good years to cover a two-year period. Our fruit trees seem a bit more erratic, with climate vagaries as influential as genetic timing. Some years apples do poorly while the pear trees have an abundance of baby pears.

With the peak of flowering in the valley coming to a close, flower and butterfly watchers will seek meadows in the mountains. Ridgetop rocky slopes and grassy openings are where you will find the greatest diversity of wildflowers and wildlife. Mountain meadows look different today than they did a century ago, when huge flocks of sheep and goats were pastured in the high Cascades. In eastern Oregon, many of the great meadows are still recovering from that overgrazing, a century later.

The largest loss of grassland ecosystems, however, has taken place in the Willamette Valley. Almost all the upland grasslands have been converted to agriculture with great loss of native flora. Most Willamette Valley grassland preserves are wet prairies with standing water in winter.

Some of the best representations of upland grassland flora are now found on roadsides and the strips of land between fields. Flowering plants that were once abundant are crowded into these linear fragments. The meadow checkermallow and the endangered peacock larkspur are two species seen in roadside strips and rarely elsewhere.

* * *

I noticed an unusual abundance of wood ducks in the eastside Delta Ponds last month. This abundance resulted in the first clutch of wood duck babies I had seen in several years. One mother wood duck has ten little ducklings scooting about!

Wildlife in the woods is as active as ever. Birds that nest in the mountain forests are migrating up the valleys and ridges. The song of the thrushes is one of my favorite sounds. In ponds frogs are leaving egg masses. The forest floor is alive with small critters, easy to find by turning over logs and rustling through the leaf litter. Millipedes are a good sign that summer is beginning.

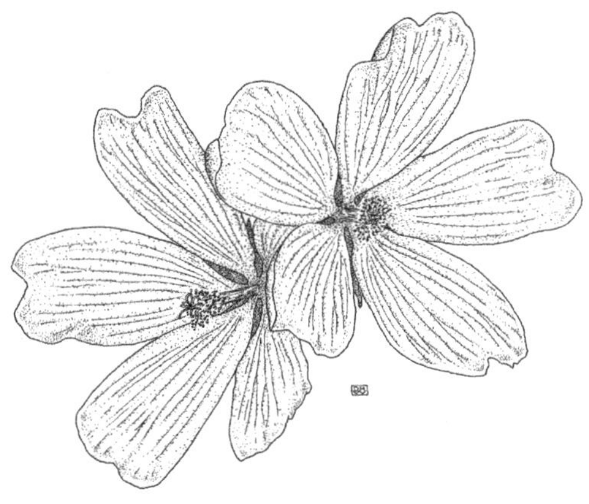

Once common, the meadow checkermallow now survives mostly in roadside strips.

As nature settles into the languorous days surrounding the summer solstice, the frenetic flowering rush of spring is tapering off. The sun rises early, before most people wake up, and sunset punctuates a late evening. For two months, the change in day length varies by barely an hour.

Meadow and woodland flowers will use the mix of long days and a reservoir of moisture in the soil to begin seed production and dispersal. Grassy hillsides transition from their brightest green to the beginning of brown over this stretch of time.

Some city streets and sidewalks take on a black, varnished appearance after several sunny days in a row. This is a sticky coating of aphid droppings. We see it mostly under oak trees, favored by aphids. Aphids will be active throughout the summer, releasing their honeydew in highest amounts on sunny days. It is harmless but a nuisance to clean off when a car is left parked under an aphid tree on a hot day.

The butterfly watching season picks up dramatically in June, if temperatures reach into the 80s a few days in a row. When a pair of swallowtail butterflies swirls by, performing their courtship dance, I stand still to watch them as long as I can.

Adelpha bredowii *is known as California sister.*

The spotted coralroot (Corallorrhiza maculata) *is an orchid that likes deep forest duff.*

July

With the passing of the solstice, wildland lovers become a bit anxious. Oh no! Gotta get in all the mountain hiking that I can before the rains come again! Snowpack is melting! Time to head for the high country!

Be patient, my friends. The melting snow means mosquitoes are breeding like crazy in snowmelt ponds. Mosquitoes are even more anxious than you about the short summer season. They must breed and lay eggs in snowmelt ponds before the ponds evaporate and before the end of summer frosts put an end to breeding frenzy.

In July the High Cascades are no fun if you have to stop to rest for a moment. Those desperate she-mosquitoes (only the girls bite—a blood meal to nurture eggs) will swarm in even if you have slathered on repellent.

Queen's cup (Clintonia) *spreads by runners on the forest floor.*

Here's a secret known to local flower watchers: The Old Cascades, the ridges west of the High Cascades, are pretty much free of mosquitoes by the end of June. Snow is long gone, open water is scarce. Head up to the Groundhog Mountain meadows or Lowder Mountain to bask in floral beauty without mosquito madness.

In the woodlands around these lower meadows, look for coral root orchids and queen's cup (*Clintonia*). Queen's cup is one of the forest floor lilies that spread by underground runners instead of a bulb or corm.

* * *

There was a slugfest in my back yard last July, and I'm not talking about fisticuffs. The slugs got the upper hand in my onion patch, taking a toll on the Walla Walla sweets. This year I have a plan, and it has to do with snakes.

I always put a tarp over the potato bed during the winter so that the summer's straw mulch will compost nicely and the bed will not be too soggy when potato planting time rolls around. During the growing season last year, I had stashed the folded tarp under some shrubbery in the corner of my yard. I had always intended to fold it tightly and store it in the shed but never got around to doing that. It stayed on the ground all summer and into the fall. When I picked it up to spread out after the potatoes had been dug, there were four or five garter snakes that slithered out. It had served as good a snake hideout as my wood pile. This spring I made a point of setting my tarp near the onion patch. I'm attracting garter snakes because they are one of the few natural predators of slugs. That's right, garter snakes eat slugs. Here's hoping they rescue my Walla Walla sweets.

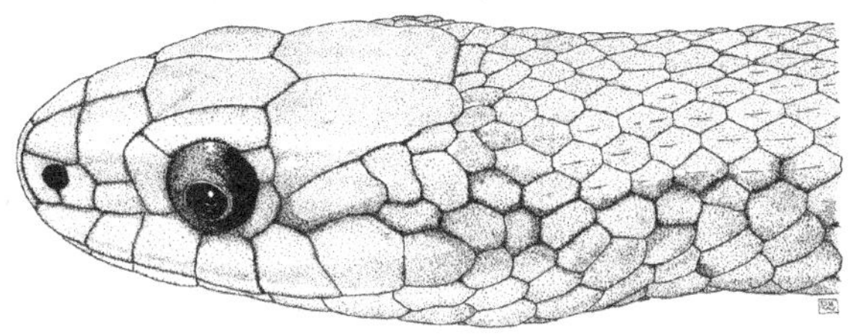

Garter snakes like to hide under tarps.

* * *

The chickadees have fledged from the nest box hanging outside our breakfast window. We miss the daily watching of their activity. It's like letting go of children who head out into the world on their own, leaving us parents. We feel a special connection to the chickadee mommy and daddy who brought tidbits of suet and bugs at a frantic rate in the final week. The end game drama was watching them coax the youngsters out of the nest by bringing a snack to the entrance hole, showing it to them, and then refusing to give it to them but instead carrying it back to the adjacent blueberry bush. It took only a day or two for the fledglings to realize the time was right to leave home.

This month, resident birds that nested early will be starting a second brood. The migratory birds completing their annual generation will hustle to fatten up and head south soon. Likewise, flying squirrel and river otter young are reaching maturity and getting prepared to explore the world for new territory. Only when they have learned to forage and hunt for themselves are

Mallard duckling.

they ready to embark. The older, wiser parents are best at the training. We watch ducks and geese doing the same.

In the lowlands, native plants are past flowering peak. Fruits are maturing. Wild cucumbers are ripening on rampant vines, its seeds often ripped untimely from the fruits by scrub jays. Wild cucumbers are a forbidden fruit to humans. Not only are they poisonous to us, but the bitter rind is just that, the most bitter plant of the region.

* * *

If you wanted to carve a dugout canoe from a log, is it better to chip out the inside first? Or should you first shape the outside and then scoop out the inside? Northwest Natives carved the sinuous lines of a canoe hull from a solid cedar log. They drilled small holes exactly to the depth of desired hull thickness, then plugged the holes with charred pegs. When an adze struck charcoal from the inside, the perfect thickness of the hull was established.

Here's another trivia question: How is a supermoon different from an ordinary full moon? Supermoon is an astrological term. The astronomical term is delicious on the tongue: syzygy at perigee. Perigee means the moon is closest to earth in its elliptical orbit so it looks fifteen percent bigger than at apogee. A full moon happens when three celestial objects line up (moon-Earth-sun). That's a syzygy. Only when a syzygy occurs at perigee do we see a supermoon.

* * *

By now the sugar snap peas in your garden should be harvested and replaced by pole beans—and the beans should be growing several inches a day.

Annuals like marigolds and zinnias are getting established in flower beds, while early lilies have their leaves withering and their bulbs enter summer dormancy. Alstroemerias (Peruvians lilies) are special: They not only brighten the garden, but they also provide cut flowers for long-lasting, colorful bouquets indoors.

Berry season is picking up pace, bringing on the tastiest two months of the year. Early strawberries are pretty much over while blueberries approach abundance. Have you ever noticed that the inside of a blueberry flower, cut in half, looks like a vegetable zombie in a robe?

Cane berries are on the way. It's time to get pie-making skills sharp for delivering marionberry, boysenberry, olallieberry or raspberry pie. By August there will be plentiful, free blackberries, both native and exotic.

We expect July to deliver a month of warm soil in the garden. There is a certain sensual pleasure gotten from dragging fingers through moist soil when weeding or planting. Bare hands, no gloves. I love it.

This is the driest month of the year in the southern Willamette Valley, so regular watering is necessary to keep the soil moist because long, hot days with ample water brings rapid growth. Fertilizer helps too, something easy to forget or put off. The best advice may be, "Fertilize weakly, weekly."

Is it really necessary to use strictly organic fertilizers? Lawn grass can't tell the difference between one source of nitrate or another; fixed nitrogen is fixed nitrogen to a plant. What about the commercial fertilizer additives? Horse manure seems pretty noble at the end of these ruminations.

* * *

Hot weather is great for bugs. Swallowtails and dragonflies dart around with incredible zip in the morning sun, their warm bodies full of energy. Spiders are getting prominent now, with dozens of little, baby spider webs all around our house. They protect us from mosquitoes. When approached they shake their webs vigorously, supposedly to make themselves appear a blur and not catchable by potential predators.

Do you like tigers and bears? The oldest carnivores around here, older than tigers, are the dragonflies. Watching dragonflies

Dragonflies are among the oldest carnivores on Earth.

gives a supreme sense of stability, reminding us that natural selection is as likely to retain a good design as it is to make a species evolve. Four hundred million years is a groove, not a rut.

* * *

If you camp in the woods this summer, take the time to learn the difference between the western red cedar and incense cedar. These two tend to occupy separate forest types. Western red cedar is more abundant to the north, all the way to Alaska. Incense cedar is much more common in the mixed hardwood/conifer forests to the south, into California. Their main region of overlap is in Lane County. Comparative drawings of the leaf scales will help you with identification. The scales of incense cedar leaves are much longer than for red cedar, three times as long as they are wide.

* * *

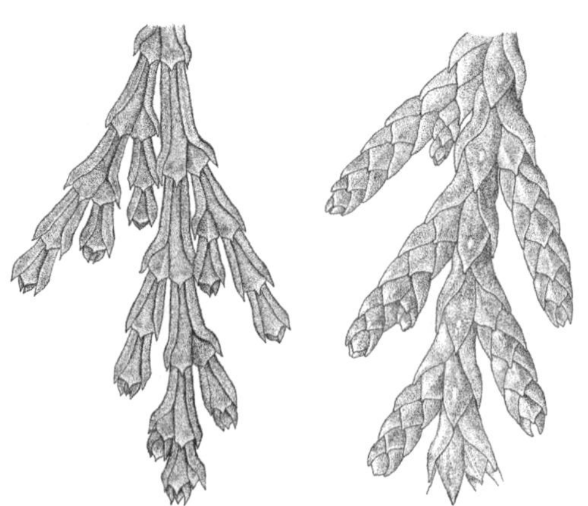

The leaf scales of incense cedar (left) are much longer than those of western red cedar (right).

The reservoirs popular with summer recreationalists are euphemistically called "lakes" by the Army Corps of Engineers. I always add "reservoir" to the names, as in "Dexter Lake Reservoir." Reservoirs are not the same water bodies as natural lakes and have distinctive ecological relationships worth remembering. Reservoirs in the Willamette River watershed were built primarily for flood control, so they are subject to dramatic changes in water level. They are always drained low in the winter. As our climate warms, high water is becoming unpredictable even in summer.

* * *

Although there has been a decline in the number of homes using firewood as a major heating source, wood heating has its advocates. Cutting up a downed tree in the front yard and stacking it to season this month saves having trucks haul it away. Stacking this month is important. All our hardwoods need a long summer protected from rain to be good quality for home heating this winter. Oak, maple, and ash that has not been split should be left a second summer to dry. Only well-dried wood burns with minimal smoke pollution.

* * *

With summer coming on strong I am drawn to mountain meadows where wildflower diversity is on glorious display. The flowering plants that dominate the meadows are relatively young in evolutionary history, only half as old as the conifers that

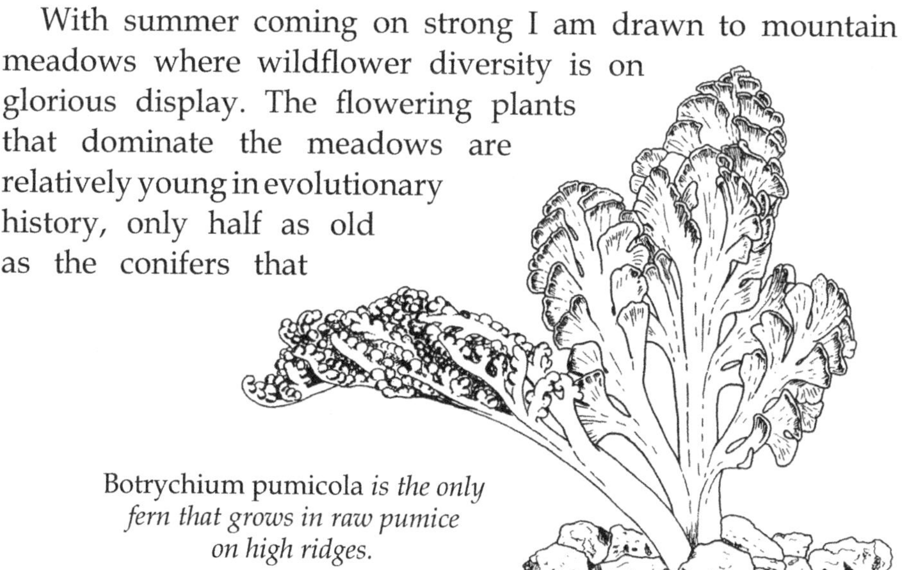

Botrychium pumicola *is the only fern that grows in raw pumice on high ridges.*

dominate our forests. The ancestry of conifers is about 300 million years, giving our forests a Paleozoic character. Liverworts and moss-like plants were the earliest land plants, their ancestors dating to over 460 million years ago. Ferns are almost as old, although most of the oldest fern families are now extinct. Modern ferns have a fossil record only about 150 million years old.

My favorites are moonworts and grape ferns, inconspicuous rare ferns that grow mostly in open meadows in our area. One species of grape fern even grows on the high-elevation pumice ridges of Cascade volcanoes. Up close, grape ferns look remarkably different from other ferns. Each plant produces a single stem every year. The stem has a fern-like leaf and a branch of spore cases that look like clusters of tiny grapes. Our biggest grape fern has an evergreen leaf that persists through a second summer. In midsummer a new shoot, looking like an embryonic brain, emerges from a womb-like pouch at the stem base.

The Sceptridium multifidum *grape fern is a magnificent sight in lakeside meadows.*

People who see me in a mountain meadow on my knees as if praying might guess I'm photographing flowers. Just as likely, I'm excited by an emerging grape fern.

The Himalayan blackberry may be an introduced invasive, but its berries are a juicy delight in August.

August

August is a berry nice month. Marionberries, boysenberries, and the cultivated blueberries pass their prime early. The mountain huckleberries get good toward the end of the month. In the valleys the invasive, poorly named Himalayan blackberry (originally from Armenia) has wonderfully juicy berries. The peak of wild blackberry picking often comes on my birthday, August 20. Earlier in August my wife and I put up a year's supply of canned peaches; it takes two days.

Luscious tomatoes and cucumbers, roots and fruits, greens and beans at the farmers' markets make this a great season to enjoy vegetarianism. If you have planted zucchini in your garden, you should be rich. A half dozen vines is like a flock of chickens; every morning you can pick three or four green "eggs." I like zucchini best when they are thumb-sized, crunchy enough to chop into a salad. If you let zucchini get too big, chop them up and freeze them. They will thicken a late winter soup.

August's warm, dry weather means you need to keep the garden watered. I'm an enthusiastic fan of hose timers controlling mini sprinklers. These allow me to set out on camping trips without fear of the garden drying out. I still have to ask neighbors to harvest my zucchini before they turn into baseball bats.

The heat of August is not always appreciated by humans, but vegetables in a well-watered garden move into high gear. A five-foot-wide trellis of pole beans will provide enough beans for an evening's meal every other day until October.

* * *

If you camp in the woods this month to seek peace and quiet, expect only the former. Even when you are far from the sounds of civilization, you will hear the background hum of millions of insects. True silence in the woods won't return until the rainy season gets under way.

Plan now for fall backpacking trips in the high country. Even after Labor Day, pink elephantshead still blooms in mountain meadows. Avoid the opening of the high Cascade rifle hunting season on the second weekend of September. The issue is not

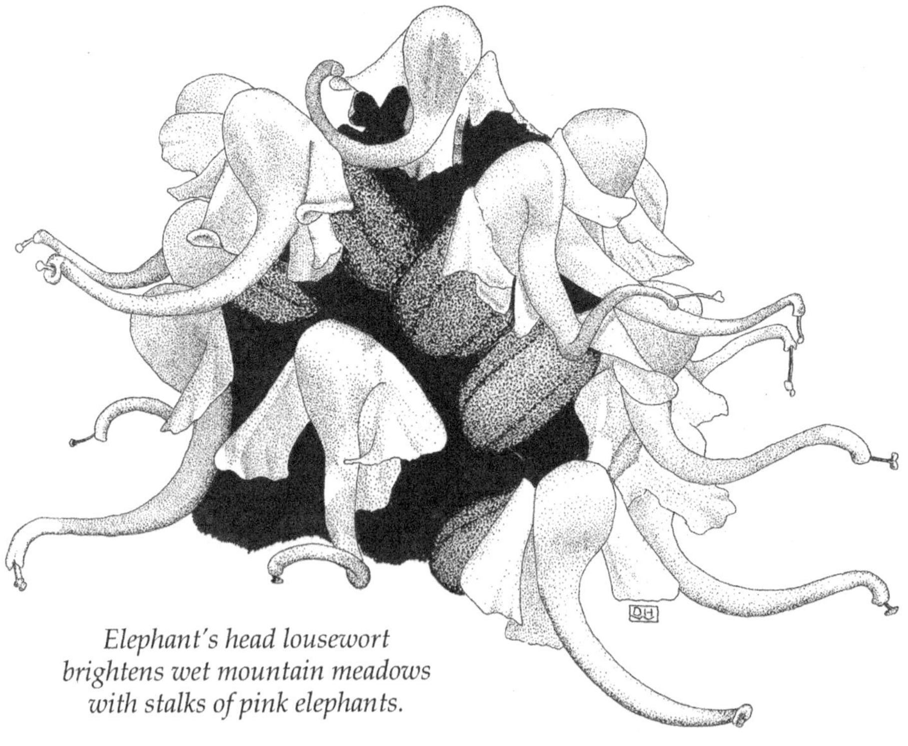

Elephant's head lousewort brightens wet mountain meadows with stalks of pink elephants.

danger from hunters; it's that all wilderness campsites will be occupied.

When camping you're likely to see little ground squirrels that are practically tame. They are so cute, coming right up to take food from your fingers. But please remember that feeding wildlife is not a good idea. In the end it harms them more than it helps.

Golden-mantled ground squirrels are healthiest if you don't give them human food.

* * *

Vines bearing pretty little purple flowers with yellow center posts are growing all over town in alleys, around ponds, and along waterways. These will develop succulent looking red berries later in the month. The plant is known as deadly nightshade and its berries are indeed poisonous. Eating even a few can make one very ill. With so many excellent wild berries starting to ripen, this is a good month to teach a child to discriminate the edible ones from the inedible.

Lakes and ponds may be reported to have a "toxic algae bloom" as waters get warm. It is unfortunate that algae are blamed for a problem caused by bacteria. The proper name for the offensive goop is cyanobacteria. The really bad population explosions look like someone has poured turquoise-tinted white latex paint in the water. This stuff is not good to drink, to wash in, or even to swim in. Maybe if we start calling it "blue green bacteria" instead of "blue green algae" the general public will kick its scientific appreciation up a notch.

Queen Anne's lace dances in open grassy areas now. Its flower buds start out in saucer formation, then bulge out like a balloon as the flowers come into full bloom. Later in the season most of these clusters will have a dark, purplish-maroon sterile flower in the middle. This is a fly decoy, a mimic that attracts flies to come and pollinate. As the seeds mature the flower cluster turns in on itself again, often harboring a spider in the urn-like center of the seed cluster.

The August full moon is a pleasure to behold. Check the calendar and gaze at the moon before bedtime. You might also plan a trip into the high country. Mountains by moonlight are magical.

* * *

Standing quietly at midday on a hillside of Scotch broom when its seed pods are ripe is like listening to a fireworks show. The drying pods gradually build tension between their two halves. When a breaking point is reached, they snap apart with a loud "pop," sending seeds in all directions. If you are in an area where invasive plants are not to be tolerated, it is a sign that you are too late for broom control this year!

My pole beans are performing as desired, snaking up the poles in right-handed spirals. I wonder if all pole beans have right-handed spirals, like standard wood screws? As Darwin noted, most species with spiral stems twist in the same way. Honeysuckle always has a left-handed twist, while grape tendrils turn to the right. Wild cucumber tendrils may seem confused, but

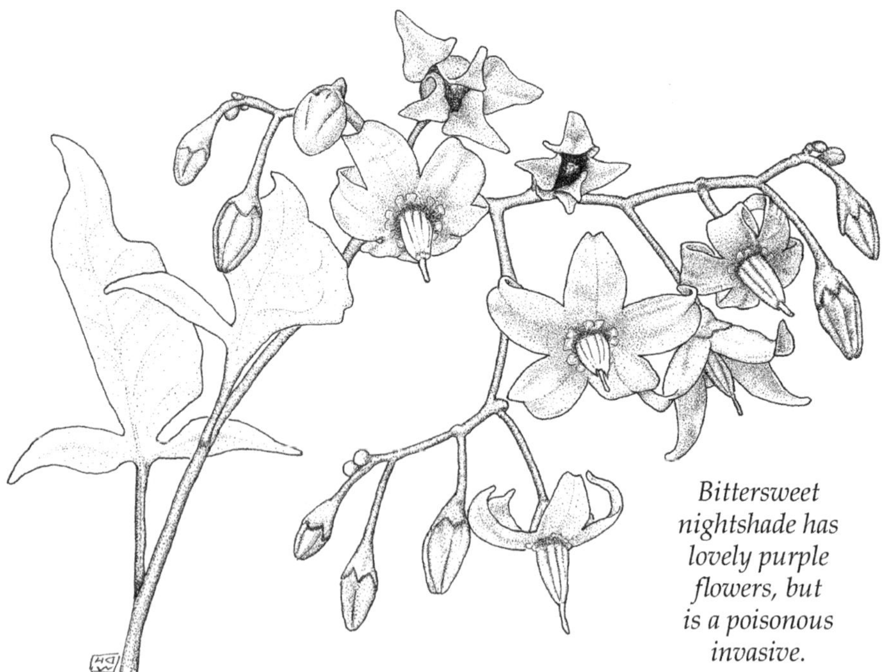

Bittersweet nightshade has lovely purple flowers, but is a poisonous invasive.

that's only because they attach at the tip first, then twist to anchor the stem. To tighten their grip, they spiral in one direction near the base and then change direction above.

The leaves of poison oak will turn bright red soon, making it easy to differentiate them from actual oaks. In the meantime, remember the adage, "Leaflets three, leave them be."

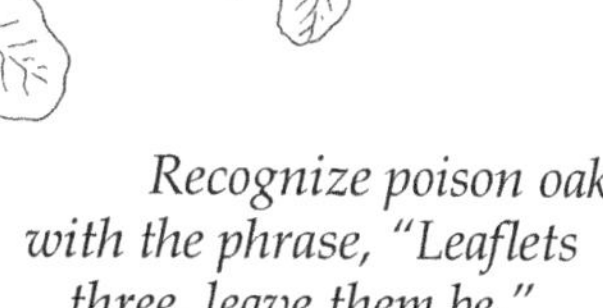

Recognize poison oak with the phrase, "Leaflets three, leave them be."

* * *

Hazelnut trees (cultivated filberts) have an abundance of swelling husks this time of year. Where the trees grow near city streets, nuts are sometimes knocked off branches by passing trucks and smashed by subsequent traffic. Squirrels and crows leap out onto the street to snatch up the soft, as yet unripe, meat of the seed inside - which we call a nut. Walnuts are also common in town, especially the Turkish walnuts that you often see

Hazelnut trees are a cultivated version of our native filberts.

in abandoned orchards and back yards. There will be lots of little walnut seedlings in flower beds next spring, planted by squirrels this fall.

* * *

One of summer's most enjoyable pastimes is wading up and down small streams, now that the water is warm and shallow. Streams that flow over gentle bedrock are especially fun. There are lots of things to see in the water, including rough-skinned newts and Pacific giant salamanders.

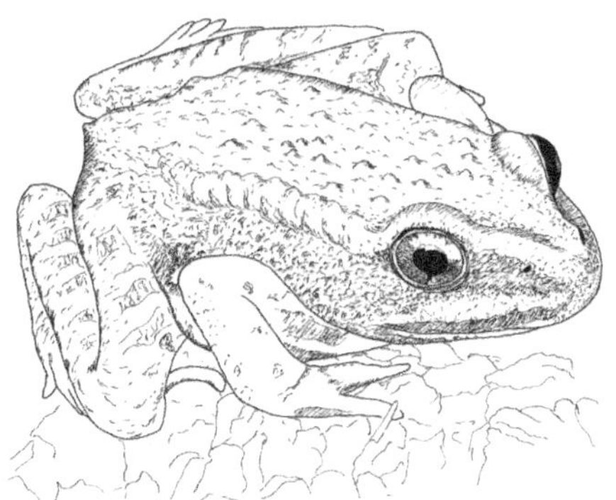

Cascade frogs may be threatened by increasing ultraviolet radiation.

Mountain meadows are now full of wildflowers and butterflies. Butterflies are as fun to watch with binoculars as birds. To fully appreciate the beauty of butterfly wings, it's important to use binocs that focus up close.

The rapidly shrinking ponds have tadpoles with legs. They must metamorphose quickly or perish!

Where there are permanent streamlets in high mountains fed by cold water springs, you often see native frogs in quiet pools. Most common is the Cascades frog. It is not a rare species but its declining numbers have become a cause for concern. Two sources of the decline are suspected. One is the spread of parasites by trout planted in high mountain lakes. The other is increased UV radiation from the sun, evidently a result of global warming.

* * *

In hot weather, gnats form small swarms in meadows near water. A typical gnat cloud is about two feet wide and three feet tall. Gnats are not fun to walk through but they don't bite. I remember my old friend, Marge Zane, showing me how to herd a swarm. She guided them here and there, slowly, with her arms spread in a wide embrace. We found that a swarm of gnats is so coherent that we could pass the cloud from one person to another. Dancing with gnats is like dancing with smoke.

* * *

A flock of nine wild turkeys showed up in our neighborhood last year. This year the flock added an astonishing total of twenty-two chicks. Early in the morning they show little fear and are easy to count. I think it is the fruit trees in our neighborhood that they like. One of the birds really stands out; its feathers are pure white, an inescapable tag that draws attention.

A teenage turkey is part of my neighborhood's increasing flock.

As the fruit gets ripe and capsules drop seeds, birds that have recently fledged are fattening up for their first migration south. Now is a good time to keep an eye on the bird feeders. Keeping them clean and full will be much appreciated by our feathered friends.

* * *

The Perseid meteor shower sends hundreds, maybe thousands, of shooting stars across the sky during the second week of August. The best meteor watching is in the hours before dawn, when the constellation Perseus rises from the northeastern horizon.

Meteors and the Milky Way are a great combination. The darkest skies for watching the show are in eastern Oregon, but because this is fire season there may be smoke.

* * *

The east side Delta Ponds are now covered with a nearly pure layer of bright green duckweed. Not only are the ducks out there shoveling it in, but geese too. It's unusual to see geese sucking duckweed. They usually prefer eating fresh grass but the grass around the ponds is so dry that the duckweed seems to be an attractive feast.

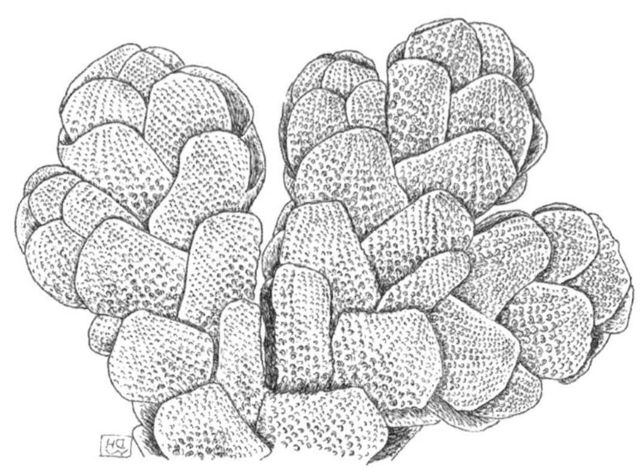

Some years the mosquito fern, Azolla, *carpets ponds with tiny reddish-purple leaves.*

The ponds have two kinds of duckweed. Common duckweed has small leaves, the size of the "o" in this sentence. But much of the green on the pond is due to water meal (*Wolffia*), an even tinier member of the flowering duckweed family. Each Wolffia plant barely exceeds size of the dot on an "i."

If you go to the Delta Ponds and find them red instead of green, you're seeing *Azolla*, the mosquito fern. This rival plant can be inconspicuous for years at a stretch. Then for a while it shoves aside the duckweed to form a dark, reddish-brown surface mat on the ponds. *Azolla* flourishes especially in winter, when it turns a lovely purple. It makes the winter migratory birds happy because it is a richer food, higher in nutrients than duckweed.

* * *

You might expect August to be the month with lowest average rainfall in our region, but that status belongs to July. The issue is the likelihood of thunderheads building up and dumping downpours in very short bursts. These towering cloud formations can be seen building up over the Cascades, sometimes over the valley, almost every August afternoon.

In this era of climate change, an increasing problem is that many thunderheads produce thunderstorms full of sound and fury but which drop very little rain. Raindrops evaporate before they hit the ground. All too often these frequently windy thunderstorms send lightning strikes across the landscape, igniting small forest fires that spread rapidly in the dry forests. More and more often, fires are restricting access to our National Forests just when hiking and camping are at their best.

Living in Eugene is a great blessing; we have so many options for interacting with nature. Even if there's smoke in the mountains and fire in the forests, we can go instead to the clear, cool air of the Coast.

* * *

A recent trip to Modoc County, south of Klamath Falls, produced one of my natural history high points of the summer. I spent a couple of mornings hiking up a steep ridge for exercise and to do some environmental art. On the highest point of the ridge is an ancient circle of stones that is reputed to have been used for vision quests in times past. The natural history prize was on the hillside below. There, a dozen big boulders had a glassy substance plastered over them. It looked as if clear opal had been splashed on them in molten form. After a bit of contemplation, I realized these were fulgerites, or what I like to call "lightningite." For some reason, perhaps a magnetic anomaly, this particular part of the slope attracted more lightning than other areas in the vicinity. When the lightning hit the top of a boulder, it melted the surface of the rock into a glassy coating. I've seen this at the top of Diamond Peak and South Sister. One might expect lightning to be attracted to the summit of peaks. That's why lookout towers are so well grounded with lightning rods. I had never seen lightning attracted to the side of a ridge before. I wonder if the people who built the vision quest circle long ago knew that this was a special place for lightning.

* * *

The nature calendar I publish notes that baby garter snakes are born in the third week of August. I forget where I got that information. One year the timing was demonstrated in my own yard. For months I had seen a big, fat, and presumably female, garter snake around our woodpile. Unlike most reptiles, momma garter snakes retain their eggs internally and bear live young. In the appropriate week, just as the calendar predicted, our yard was filled with baby garter snakes.

So small and cute! Barely five inches long, they seemed to be everywhere. I was redoing rock work in our garden and found them under every other rock. It was clear they were of the same litter; they all appeared at the same time and were exactly the same size. Right away they set to work hunting for tasty invasives. I kept one baby snake to photograph and fed it an earthworm, which it ate without hesitation. When they're bigger, I expect them to get to work on my garden's slugs.

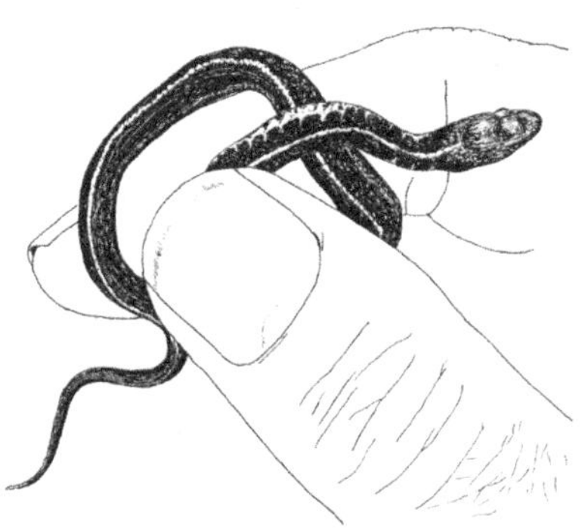

Baby garter snakes crept out into my garden right on time.

September

September is the time of the year when the aroma of lightly fermented blackberries is carried on a warm breeze during my evening walks by the Delta Ponds. That smell identifies the season, late summer in southern Willamette Valley, when our account of fine days is well stocked.

The equinox, usually around September 22, is reflected in shorter days. The rate of change itself changes. The day-to-day change at equinox is about 3 minutes a day but only 30 seconds a day at winter solstice.

Gardens are bountiful this month, and require little attention beyond watering and harvesting. My best producers are pole beans and cherry tomatoes. Peaches are done. If you don't already practice preservation, this is a good year to learn. Simply chopping and freezing in zipper bags works for most garden produce.

One wild berry that's still accessible is the thimbleberry. Shaped like a bright red thimble, these berries are still abundant along lower forest roadsides. Yes, it takes an hour to gather enough for jam, but it's worth it.

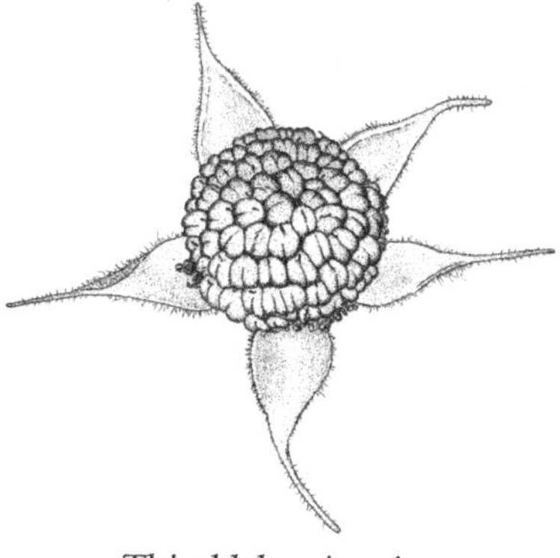

Thimbleberries ripen in September.

Winter may be far off but the natural world is anticipating its arrival. Roosevelt elk and deer are bugling and fighting for the right to

Male black-tailed deer become agressive in fall, jostling for the right to procreate.

procreate. Their offspring will be born in the spring. Western long-eared bats will enter winter hibernation in the mountains. Insects gather pollen and nectar to store in hives or nests that will nurture the next generation. Reptiles are at their time of most rapid growth. With body temperature controlled by the environment, high activity in warm weather allows fattening up for the cool winter months to follow.

Most of the native flowers have long since finished blooming but the leafy beggarticks (*Bidens*) reach peak bloom this month. It reflects their affinity for wet places that dry out at the end of the season. Their serrated leaflets are so similar to cannabis it occasionally fools people into thinking they have found escaped marijuana.

* * *

Squirrels and scrub jays are now busily burying hazelnuts and acorns. The indigenous peoples of this area never did use acorns much, but their middens are filled with wild hazelnut shells. It is a marvel that they were able to find enough for a harvest. Nuts seem scarce on wild hazelnuts, and competition with squirrels and birds must be tough.

I grump when squirrels dig in my otherwise tidy flowerbeds to bury their treasures. The jays do the same thing but with more finesse, simply hammering nuts into the ground like pile drivers.

Some Septembers bring a massive production of California black oak acorns but not Oregon white oak. Other years it's the opposite. Some years neither species seems to have many acorns. Known as masting, the occasional overproduction of acorns means that squirrels and jays can't use them all. In those years more acorns are buried than eaten. Popular lore maintains that squirrels forget where some were buried and those germinate to produce seedlings. The truth is they don't have a bad memory; seedlings abound when hawks thin the squirrel population. All the acorns buried by the missing squirrels are free to grow.

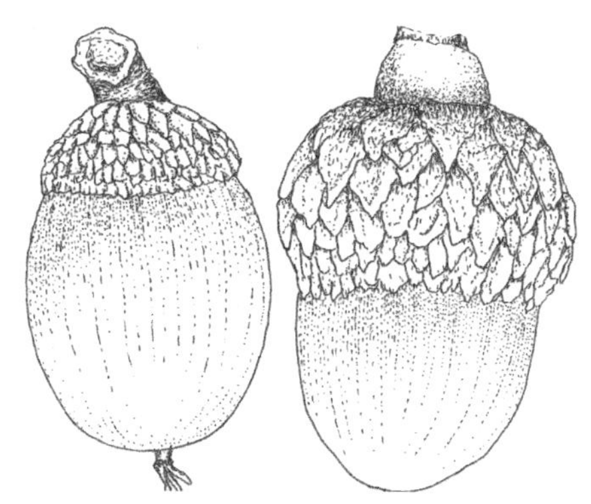

We have two kinds of native oaks, with two kinds of acorns.

* * *

Mild winters and dry, late summers classify us as having a Mediterranean climate. Wild yearly variation is normal. This month, at the end of our dry season, river and pond levels get very low. I imagine the herons like it very much because all the little fish which have been reproducing so prolifically all summer get concentrated in shallow places. Fish are easy to catch, and herons fatten up before slim fishing in the cold months.

Birds are getting restless and migration is stirring in their bones—hollow bones evolved for long-distance flight. Mid-month thousands of Vaux's swifts will stop in Eugene for a week or so on their southward migration. They roost in huge numbers in the old chimney of Agate Hall, at 17th and Agate. It is a sight to see them swirling in the evening sky by the thousands, then swooping together down into the chimney moments after sunset.

Like birds, seeds are on the move. The ones with tiny, barbed hairs may be the most noticeable. They bind tightly to socks and twist up tough knots in long-haired dogs. These are known as hitchhikers. Other seeds use temptation for dispersal, being buried in a fleshy coating that attracts birds like robins and cedar waxwings. The birds swallow the fruits and then deposit the seeds far and wide.

* * *

Insects are getting ready for overwintering, laying eggs or burrowing into the ground to pupate. Spiders are catching the last and fattest of these insects for the same reason: making egg-nests to overwinter. Fat spiders mark summer's end.

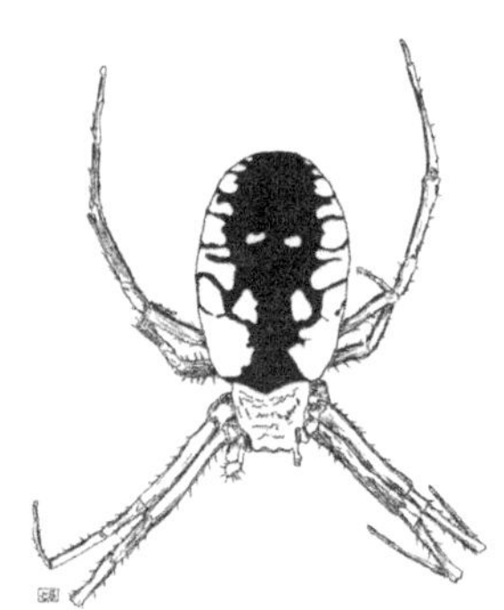

The Argiope *spider feasts on insects to lay eggs.*

I learned about a new garden pest this summer: the assassin bug. I should be happy it is in my garden because it is a predator that hunts the vegetable pests. Its dark side is that it is a blood sucker, like ticks and mosquitoes. Baby assassin bugs, called nymphs, are under a quarter of an inch long. I caught one on my wrist when I felt a stinging. Wiping it off left a blood smear. A few days later the site turned into a swollen, itchy welt. One got me under my ear lobe. Because I scratched too much, the welt made my lobe swell up and redden. How we gardeners suffer!

* * *

This is the best time of the year to go up into the mountains. The likelihood of sunny weather is most reliable, the mosquitoes and tourists are gone, the snow banks have withdrawn from trails and camp spots, the mornings are crisp, and the days lovely from dawn to dusk.

The dry weather of September can also heighten fire danger, so it's a good season to try backpacking like John Muir, with no fires or stoves at all, just nuts and dried fruits. And, to be contemporary, corn chips, energy bars, and cookies. You'll travel lighter, too, without the cooking gear.

The golden deer fly can annoy hikers in the mountains.

I had an enlightening experience on a recent camping trip. We were in a large campground where firewood has to be purchased in bundles of fairly large chunks. A hatchet or axe is needed to split off some kindling to start a fire. The first morning, I heard a loud "thwack-thwack" soon after daylight. I was brought to a full awakening with a resentful thought. "What idiot is chopping wood this early in the morning?" It kept up for over twenty minutes, so I stumbled out to seek the campers who were so rude. My resentfulness turned to amusement when I discovered the thwacks were from Douglas-fir cones being cut by squirrels from tall trees. The cones were dropping onto the roof of the campground restroom with a bang. I went back to bed, pleased that there was nobody to be mad at; here was simply a sound of nature to accept gracefully.

* * *

I look forward to the annual surge of migratory bird sightings. Already my bird feeders are swamped with flocks of goldfinches, chickadees, bushtits, and sparrows. Their fledglings add to the flurry around the suet cages and feeders. It is a delight to watch the fuzzy teenagers figuring out how to land gracefully. The adults also teach them to build up energy for migration—and not to stay in one spot for too long, in order to avoid the attention of predatory hawks.

At the Delta Ponds, ducklings and goslings are now almost as big as the adults, capable of foraging on their own. It took me some years before I recognized that mallard drakes look like

White-crowned sparrows return to bird feeders in September.

mallard hens for most of their first year. Juvenile great blue herons can also trick the birdwatcher. For their first year they look like oversized green herons.

* * *

Rain or not, mushroom season is here. Chanterelles are already up near the coast. Porcini in the mountains will have to wait for next month's rains.

October

According to some traditions, October is the month the gods take vacation, so it behooves us to see that sacred places are kept secure and tidy. As the gods have taken care of our surroundings, we must help take care of theirs.

Autumn rains usually begin blowing down from the north this month, carried in on cold air. That produces the fall color we enjoy, most of the reds coming from vine maple and poison oak. In good years the bigleaf maple turns a lovely yellow gold.

As maple leaves turn yellow, notice that some have little green islands with black spots. This is the tar spot fungus (*Rhytisma punctatum*), a living antibiotic hosted inside the maple leaves. The fungus lives inside the leaves, unnoticed, all year. Its symbiotic function, theory holds, is providing endogenous antiviral security, similar to *Penicillium*. Tar spot fungus becomes visible only at the end of the season, when it borrows a small piece of the leaf's food factory to reproduce. The fungus is preserving the last of the green leaf cells to produce spores for the next season. The green ring around each colony

Bigleaf maples host the tar spot fungus, a natural antibiotic.

does that job. The tiny black spots, building a low dome in the center of origin, are the spore cases for next year's cohabitation.

Parasites and symbionts like the gall wasps on oaks and tar spot fungi in bigleaf maple wait out their dormant stage in decaying leaves on the ground. If the leaves get raked up in fall, their life cycle is broken.

* * *

This is the time of the year when mushrooms capture my attention. While the cold air is shutting down deciduous trees and flowering herbs, the rain is stimulating the fungi under the forest canopy into action.

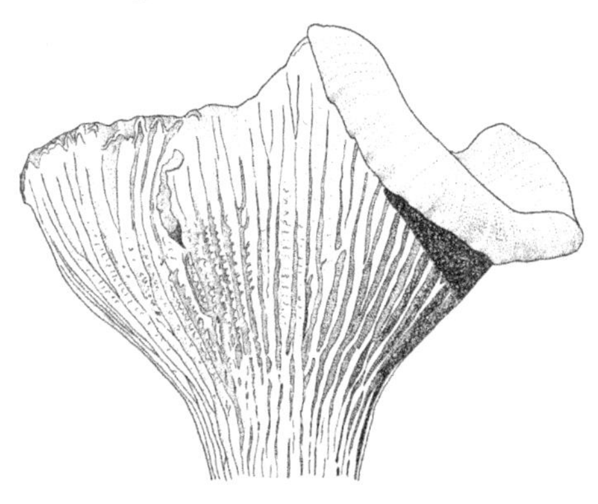

It's time for chanterelle mushrooms!

I love mushrooms. Not only are they fascinating organisms, but they also provide some of my favorite gastronomic treats. A favorite of the region, the golden chanterelle, reaches peak production in October. Only if fall rains arrive in good order will it be a good year for chanterelles. My dentist, an avid mushroom hunter, remembered a year when there were so many chanterelles in the woods that he met very few commercial pickers. The explanation is that when there's a glut of chanterelles on the market, the prices paid by buyers are low. Low prices keep the commercial pickers out of the way of the rest of us.

A good mushroom year also portends a great mushroom show. The Mushroom Festival, held on the last Sunday of October, is one of two major natural history events of the year at Mount Pisgah Arboretum south of Springfield. The Eugene Natural History Society always has a booth at this event to publicize our lectures. We display curious objects from nature to look at and, more importantly, to touch. The "Please Touch" table was an invention of Society member Dave Stone. It was popular from the beginning and continues to be so. I am curator of the boxes of material we use for our display. I'm always looking for new items to put out.

Sitting at the table and talking to interested folks may not seem as exciting as hunting mushrooms in the woods, but it is also a pleasant way to enjoy natural history with curious kids.

The fried chicken mushroom has a slight radishy taste.

* * *

Our autumn is what Zen tradition calls "Seeds to Snow." Because we share a north temperate climate with Japan, that designation fits us well. It's time to pull out summer garden plants and put in seeds and starts for the winter garden.

Gardeners expect October to usher in the rainy season, but some years sunshine keeps tomatoes and grapes ripening right up to the end of the month. Even if the rains begin early, I've found it is possible to ripen tomatoes by moving the entire vine into the shed. I uproot a tomato plant, shake off the dirt, prune lanky branch tips, and hang it upside down in a cool storage room. So long as it doesn't freeze in there, the tomatoes will continue to ripen nicely. They are less likely to rot on hanging vines than if picked and spread on newspapers.

* * *

I love late season butterflies, especially little golden-brown skippers. They are especially noticeable around fall blooming asters. There are two that might show up in your garden in October, the sachem skipper and the woodland skipper.

The woodland skipper butterfly visits gardens in fall.

* * *

Returning from a walk with burrs in my socks and our dog's fur demonstrates that seed dispersal is under way. Seeds have been waiting for the onset of the rainy season. Conifers have begun showering huge rains of seeds from their cones. Only a tiny percent of these seeds are actually viable. The conifers' strategy is to deceive seed eaters into thinking all cones are empty, so they won't spend time picking through the empties to find the good ones. This strategy doesn't stop determined squirrels. In late summer cones are cut down by squirrels and hidden under logs to be recovered and eaten later. In the woods you see piles of cone scales at the end of big logs, where squirrels have enjoyed "cone on the cob."

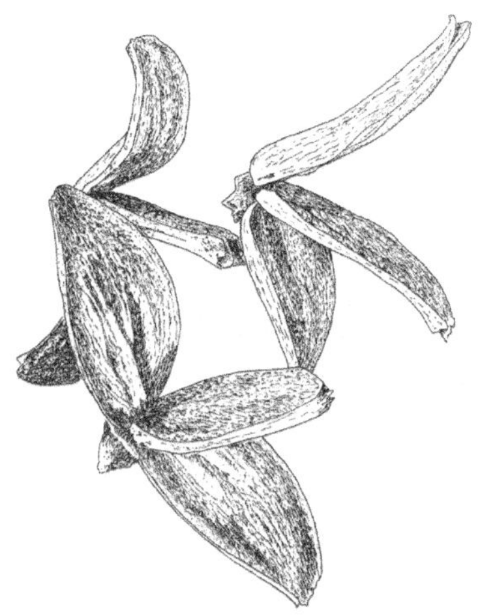

Incense cedar cones look like the bill of a long-tongued duck.

Douglas-fir cones that the squirrels overlook will remain on the trees long after the seeds are shed. Then they fall to the ground and slowly rot. The cones of incense cedar come raining down in October as soon as their seeds are scattered to the winds. It's easy to recognize incense cedar's one-inch-long cones because their curved halves curl out like the bill of a quacking cartoon duck.

The cones of true firs, including noble fir and subalpine fir, disintegrate from top down. Their scales and seeds fall separately, a few at a time. Eventually just the cone's core remains as a little spire atop a branch.

* * *

In our culture, Halloween is the gateway to winter, a time of wet, cold days and long nights. Humans have a tendency to get glum during our rainy season, cowering inside until the spring equinox. Most of our forest trees are evergreen conifers that find winter a wonderful time. With plenty of moisture to keep stomates open, they photosynthesize at a steady rate all winter.

Deciduous broadleaf trees miss out on this winter activity. Without leaves they cannot photosynthesize. But the mosses on their branches dance with delight, awakened from their summer desiccation dormancy. With extra light and moisture, the moss turns a brighter green as new growth appears at the tips of their stems.

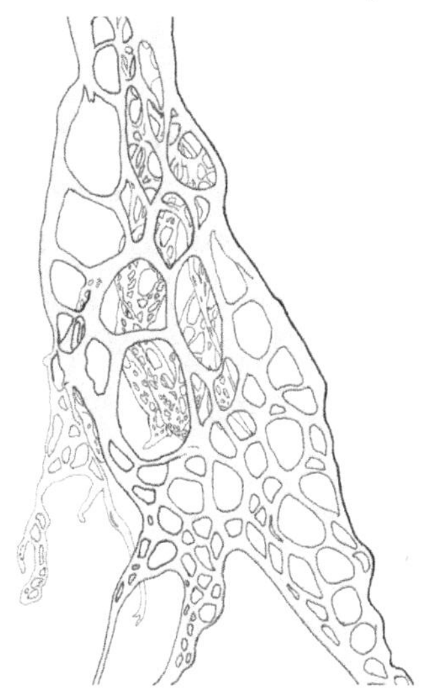

Fishnet lichen hangs like cobwebs on Halloween.

Lichens often cover the outer parts of oak and ash branches. As with mosses, this is the start of their main growing season. The growth form of lichens is more varied than mosses. All mosses have tiny stems with tiny leaves, but lichens form ribbons, tubes, bushes and swags. Lichens also come in more colors than mosses. Weavers know that lichens can be used to make dyes for coloring cloth. Some of the best colors are hidden, exposed only when the lichen is fermented.

Lesser goldfinches molt in October.

If you stroll the riverbank path at Mount Pisgah you'll see long, pendulous lichens that look like Spanish moss. These are fishnet lichens, a nice cobwebby Halloween sight.

* * *

Little birds are crowding our feeders as if we were the only source of suet and finch seed in the neighborhood. They are molting right now, so they have fresh flight feathers for safe migration, more fluff for warmth, and less color to avoid notice by predators. Sunflower seed chunks seem to be particularly desirable.

What remains of the pole beans can be left to finish maturing before drying for next year's planting.

As soon as the rains come, we can plant our winter greens. They grow slowly but have fewer pests than spring-planted salad. Gardens will keep producing until the first frost, slowly but steadily. One of the reasons I plant zinnias is that they keep getting stronger and brighter right up to that first hard freeze.

* * *

A rainless October gives me a sense of unease. Even where there are no fires, the woods are so dry that there is a "wrong" smell in the air. It's especially disturbing for people who practice shinrin-yoku, forest bathing or forest breathing. Good research has demonstrated that time spent in nature is good for one's mental wellbeing, but I have a suspicion that the opposite can be true if the forest "feels" threatened. Something is not right, and a sensitive person can smell it. I look forward to rain in fall. Not only does it put out fires, it will give us the sense—smell—that the seasons are back on track. A wet forest smell is as recognizable as the smell of a wet dog. And much more wonderful.

* * *

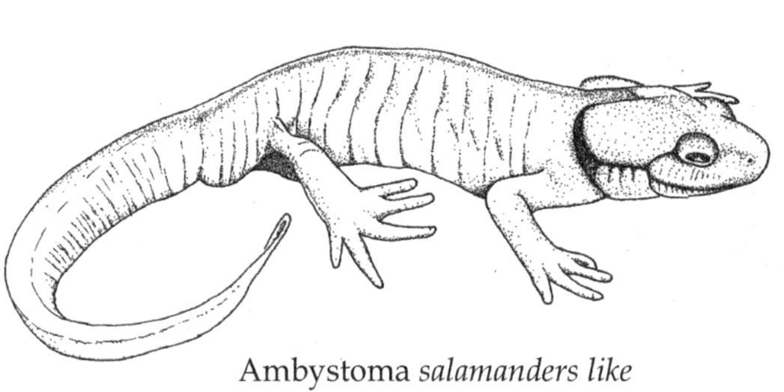

Ambystoma *salamanders like to live under rotting logs.*

When the rains arrive, logs on the forest floor swell with moisture. Mosses and liverworts that rely on moist conditions love those big, rotting logs. Logs like this never completely dry out, so they are special to many kinds of woodland critters. Salamanders live underneath. Tree seedlings sprout on top, glad for the moisture and nutrition. The mosses there will be happy all winter.

* * *

Science magazine reports that the bird population of North America has declined by about 3 billion over the past fifty years. Songbirds have been hit the hardest, while raptors and waterfowl are actually increasing. The causes include climate change, pesticides, urbanization, and habitat degradation. All of these together are evidence that humans may be committing suicide by ecocide.

I have a theory that borders on the metaphysical. Perhaps one of the causes of our breakdown of civil society is distancing from nature. Distancing is both subliminal (like urbanites not having access to forests to breathe or enjoy) and intellectual (like not recognizing we are part of nature). We originated from nature, as did every other living being. Environmental decay is the driver of distancing and, according to some thinkers, always has moral consequences.

November

November is the month to drain and roll up the garden hoses. A sudden hard frost, which can happen with little warning, will also ruin your garden's watering timers, so bring them indoors too. Be prepared to wrap outside faucets. It wouldn't hurt to give plants in the yard one final, gentle feeding of fertilizer.

White-crowned sparrows sing to claim territory.

We can enjoy a few more days of marigolds, zinnias and other annual flowers that are just past their peak production.

Bird lovers will be keeping a close eye on their feeders. This time of the year there are impressive flocks of small birds, which have come down from the mountains to feed on grains. They love to congregate in yards that have water and different kinds of feed. Water gets to be very important when temperatures drop below freezing. Investing in a watering bowl that keeps the water thawed would be a great holiday gift to your feathered friends.

Pine siskins are always in flocks.

* * *

Like most warblers, the Townsend's warbler has yellow and black markings.

Leaves of our broadleaf trees don't finish falling until late November. A few bright orange leaves still cling to bigleaf maples. Alder leaves just turn brown and fall quickly. These fallen leaves will decompose and add their nutrients back into the soil. These recycled nutrients will, in turn, enhance the growth of leaves next spring.

Different plants decompose in different ways. I like the way Oregon ash leaves break down. By late winter their soft tissues will have disappeared completely but the fine mesh-like skeleton is preserved in minute detail. The stems of big herbs show their circulatory system as they decay. The way a leaf connects to a stem is revealed as an intricate web.

* * *

Notice that winter annuals have already sprouted. Some of these small plants are natives, but in town the exotic ones are ubiquitous. Look for patches of common chickweed. Until it begins blooming sometime in late January, chickweed is a fine green. Its fresh, nutty flavor is a treat. A single line of hairs up the stem distinguishes it from any other weed. Just beware of foraging where herbicides might have been used.

As broadleaf trees drop their leaves, mosses and ferns on the tree trunks have greened up. Watch the spore cases develop on licorice ferns. They are clustered in white dots this month. As spores mature, the dots will become bright yellow mounds. After spores are shed in early spring, the mounds turn brown.

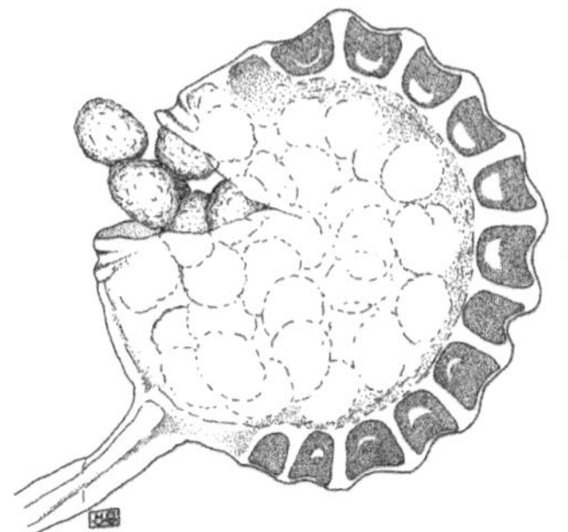
A sword fern's spore case.

Sword ferns on the ground appear to be doing nothing. Their new fronds came up last spring and shed spores in late summer. However, they are storing energy all winter, the advantage of being evergreen. If you have too-large sword ferns in your yard, you can dwarf them by cutting the fronds now. New fronds will be only two thirds as long next year.

* * *

The rainy season has begun. You can see it in the hundreds of thousands of tiny seedlings that are appearing on what has been bare ground for months. They are still so small that the ground looks bare. I have to look closely to see the hordes of double green pinheads. Things like bedstraw and bittercress have a pair of seed leaves, called cotyledons. They were already present in miniature inside the seed. With only tiny cotyledons showing, it's too early to tell exactly what plant they are. The first pair of true leaves has to sprout before you know for sure.

Grass seedlings are easier to recognize. They send up a single, tiny, green spear. That's why members of the grass family are known as monocotyledons while those families with two seed leaves are called dicotyledons. Conifers are different; hemlock seeds have up to six cotyledons.

* * *

The walnut trees are dropping walnuts. Actually, squirrels are up in the tree cutting walnuts off and letting them fall to the ground. Then they retrieve them and either bury them or sit on the fence gnawing loudly, "Ch-ch-ch-ch-ch-ch-ch," until they get into the interior. I've seen as many as six or seven squirrels tending the same tree. These are eastern fox squirrels. They're not

Crows are so intelligent that they wait for cars to run over walnuts, cracking the shells.

native but then neither are the walnuts.

Crows like the walnuts, too. They quite happily steal the walnuts cut down by the squirrels. Squirrels are not at all quiet about expressing their dismay. Crows can't chew open the walnuts, so they carry them away to deal with them. I saw one trying to beat a walnut on the corner of somebody's roof. When that didn't work, it flew up in the air and dropped the walnut in the street. A much better idea, like gulls dropping clams on the rocks along the ocean shore.

Crows are smart. I've noticed them hanging around a walnut tree that hangs over the street. They are waiting for cars to drive over the nuts, smashing the hull and releasing the meat for easy picking. Then the crows just have to beat the squirrels to the feast – and watch out that they don't get run over themselves.

* * *

Mushrooms are everywhere. In lawns you'll see clusters or "fairy rings" of whitish agarics. Most of these are in the group that David Arora calls the "lose your lunch bunch." They may look like the mushrooms in grocery stores, but they are almost certainly inedible.

Recently I saw a nice patch of birch tree boletes in a lawn. They are edible and looked very good but I refused to pick them because the lawn had clearly been maintained with weed killer.

*King boletus (*Boletus edulus*) is one of the few edible and delicious boletes.*

The toxins were likely to be concentrated in the mushrooms. I'll wait and gather wild mushrooms in the woods.

One cream-colored fungus to look for in the forest is the delicious oyster mushroom. It likes decaying alder logs.

* * *

November is a good month to think about going to the Oregon coast for an autumnal adventure. Except around the major holidays, off season rates invite locals to enjoy staying in a favorite bed and breakfast or resort hideaway.

Snow is likely to arrive in the high country this month. Like October rain, November snow is unpredictable. Some years Thanksgiving vacation is for skiing, some years it's for hiking. We can expect McKenzie Pass to close for the season and for Crater Lake to enter its winter mode, attracting cross-country skiers instead of mountain bikers.

* * *

Newts will have gotten down to their favorite ponds to breed by now. Males arrive first and wait for the ladies. Egg laying will take place before long and the young larvae will emerge in late winter or early spring. They may take two seasons to mature. Slow moving, they appear vulnerable to any hungry predator. Newt skin contains a virulent toxin, however, and they defend themselves by showing their bright yellow belly and curled tail underside that says, "stay away." Swallowing a single newt is enough to kill a man.

* * *

Some of the black cottonwoods along the Willamette River have dropped their leaves completely while others are still laden with green leaves. Their variance seems greater than for any other tree species. A good project for a family with kids would be to pick a line of cottonwoods and take pictures once a week through the season, noting when each tree turns color and when it becomes bare. Are the early leaf droppers in autumn the earliest to leaf out in spring?

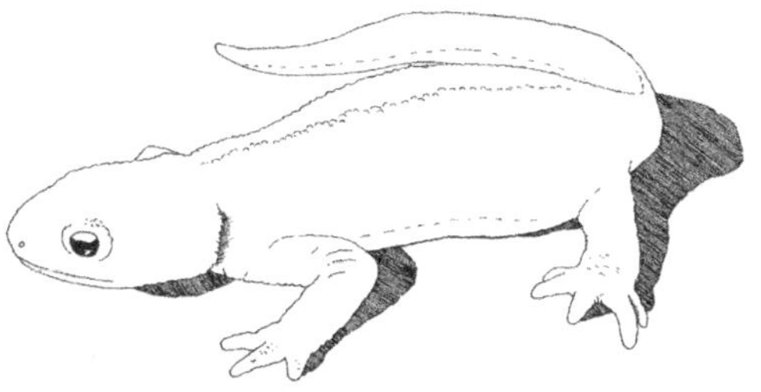

The orange skin of a rough-skinned newt is a warning that it is highly toxic.

Aspen, in the same genus as cottonwood, grows in clones. A hillside of aspen will have some clusters with yellow leaves, some with green leaves. Watch for this if you travel to southeast Oregon's mountains.

* * *

American wigeons are back in the Delta Ponds. I believe these are the first of our winter migrants to arrive. I look forward to the increasing diversity of waterfowl. On our side of the Delta Highway we have had only mallards and Canada geese for a long time.

There are still a few turtles by the ponds, but it appears the cormorants have taken over their favorite sunning logs. With increasing

Mallards live here year-round, but most other ducks migrate.

cold weather and less sun showing, turtles will burrow into the mud at the bottom of the ponds to brumate.

* * *

Now that summer is over, old needles are falling from Douglas-firs in great numbers. These are last year's needles for the most part. The needles that emerged from their buds this spring will finally get around to doing their job. Over the rainy season they will double in thickness, storing carbohydrates. When the weather gets warmer in the spring, they will transport that energy down to the tree trunk and put on some board feet.

* * *

Working in the garden along the street creates opportunity to talk to neighbors who walk by. It is interesting how folks seem comfortable asking about what I'm growing or comment on the nice pea trellis I have. It would seem that gardening in front of your home is a basic, ancient form of social media.

* * *

Our nasturtiums are going crazy this fall, sprawling vigorously over the garden beds where cucumbers used to grow. Cucumbers, like the zucchini, succumbed to mildew soon after the rains began. The nasturtiums' success allows us to enjoy little, edible bouquets that last a few days inside.

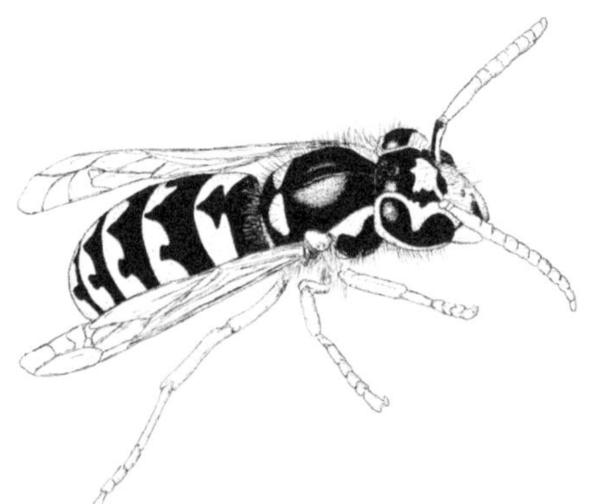

Yellowjackets are native to Oregon, yet don't mind pollinating invasive ivy.

* * *

Among the most noxious, aggressive, non-native plants is English ivy. It has been widely used as an easily established ground cover. I suppose English ivy will continue to be used in landscaping, despite its tendency to escape and overwhelm the understory of woodlands in urban parks. One of its odd traits is to bloom in late fall, providing a nectar source when little else is available. Honeybees love it. A surprise is how many native pollinators swarm flower clusters—yellowjackets, wasps, and even some evening moths.

* * *

Our house doors are working again. The drought of summer had dried out the upland soil beneath our house. As the clay shrank the corners of our house settled, causing door jambs to warp and doors to stick. The rainy season has rehydrated the clay, making it expand. The sudden release of doors that had been sticking was dramatic this November.

* * *

An old-fashioned way to enjoy fall is to press and dry leaves for art projects. A stack of newspapers under a weighted board is all the equipment needed. Gather leaves that catch your fancy and put them between folded newspaper sections, press under a board with heavy weight. Swap out moist newspapers with dry ones every day until the leaves are dry, usually a week or less.

* * *

The first hard freeze of the year typically happens around now. Tender garden flowers like zinnias and dahlias get frost bitten and suddenly turn to mush overnight.

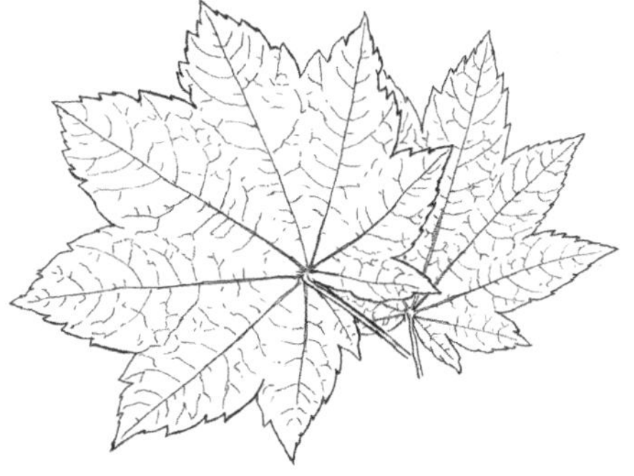

Try pressing the red leaves of vine maple for fall decorations.

Come the end of the month, native perennial herbs like cow parsnip, meadow rue, tall larkspur, and nonnative poison hemlock emerge from summer dormancy. Their folded leaves will unfurl slowly all winter, taking advantage of sunlight through the leafless trees overhead to get a head start on the bloom of the coming spring.

December

December is the rainiest month of the year in the Willamette Valley. Outside it is wet, cold, and still, with nothing much happening. Or so you'd think. The illusion of stillness in winter is betrayed by the steady, hidden pulse of regeneration. Remarkable things are happening. Great horned owls are breeding, salmon are spawning, mosses are making new shoots, and gray whales are headed south.

Millions and millions of insects are undergoing metamorphosis. Insects in pupa stage are hiding out underground, in fallen leaves, in tree bark crevices, in cocoons hanging under branches or in the cracks of your house siding. Inside their pupal shells the innards of caterpillars and grubs have turned into an amorphous jelly. Like magical shape shifters, when they are ready to emerge next spring their bodies will have been transformed into walking,

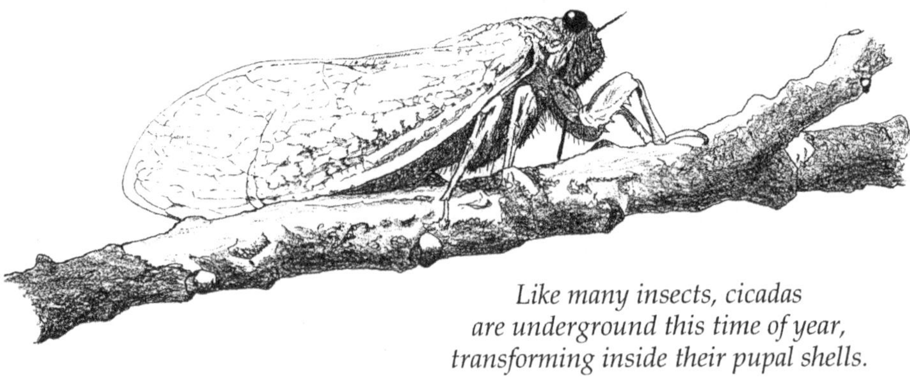

Like many insects, cicadas are underground this time of year, transforming inside their pupal shells.

flying, buzzing adults.

Transformation is also happening in every plant. Douglas-fir needles are getting fat. Winter annuals such as bittercress, bedstraw, and chickweed have already sprouted. Cut open a woody plant bud and you'll see partly formed leaves and flowers. In time, flowers will spring forth when buds burst. But quietly now they grow, each part forming in tight symmetry.

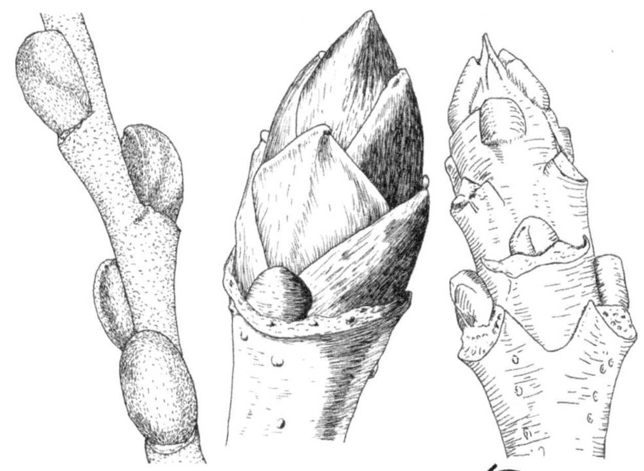

Tree buds fatten in winter. From left to right: ash, maple, and willow.

Share this wonder with a friend or family member. Have a botanist friend show you some osoberry, also known as "Indian plum". Every two weeks or so, pick some buds and cut them open, examining the contents with a hand lens. Make sketches, take photos, note weather, keep a nature diary. Be the first to see osoberry bloom!

* * *

When a cold front swoops down the Willamette Valley, everything had better be prepared for it. For wild animals, it means having a source of food carefully stashed away—and the ability to stay dormant until it's warm enough to dig up that stash. This is why squirrels bury nuts.

Out in the forests, mountain beavers have their hay stored underground. They cut their favorite herbage and spread it out to dry before hauling it into their dens.

For plants, there is no option for sudden reaction, no ability to quickly run and huddle underground. Their dormancy has been developing for a long time. Trees and shrubs that drop their leaves start forming winter buds in summer, and by December their primordial leaves have started to enlarge inside the buds, just like the embryos of pregnant bears hibernating in dens.

Herbaceous perennials have mostly retreated underground, often long before the cold season arrived. Often their aboveground parts withered and vanished in July. Their buds are on short stems that overwinter at or below the surface of the soil. A thick mulch of leaves would be nice.

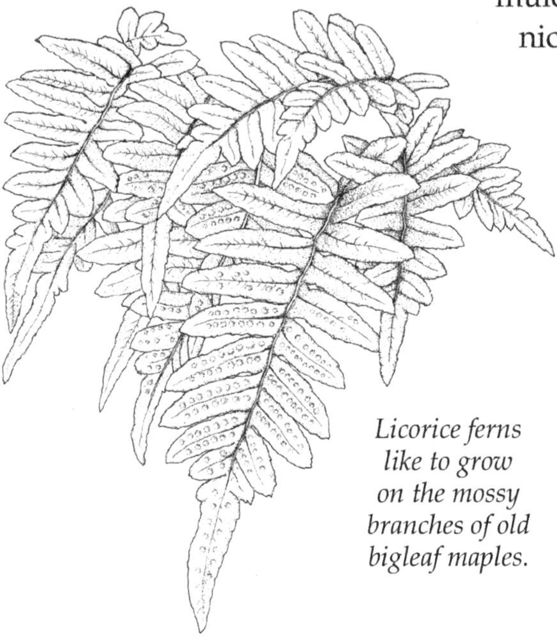

Then there are the perennial, evergreen plants. These are ones that keep their green leaves throughout the winter. Their leaves are tough enough to withstand freezing, yet stay alive and strong through early spring. My favorites are ferns, like sword fern and parsley fern.

Licorice ferns like to grow on the mossy branches of old bigleaf maples.

* * *

I can see Orion back in the evening sky when I take our dog out for our bedtime stroll. Orion and the Pleiades are old friends returning from a six-month voyage to the other side of the world. If the sky is clear before dawn in the middle of the month, you may be able to see the Geminid meteor shower.

Newly uncurled fronds of licorice ferns on tree branches are wonderful to behold. Their bright, spring green is magical at a time of the year when most terrestrial herbaceous plants are withered and dormant. I counted how many sporangium clusters are on a typical leaf and how many spore cases in a typical cluster. Then I multiplied the result by 64, the number of spores in a sporangium. The average production of a licorice fern is nearly 5 million spores per frond!

* * *

Darkness comes early in December, now that midwinter is upon us. The solstice, when the length of days starts increasing again, usually arrives four days before Christmas. Long nights are going to be around for a couple of months. I treasure clear, chilly nights when the stars put on a show from early in the evening. I mark the yearly cycle with only one constellation: Orion. Three bright stars decorate his belt. The sword hanging at an angle below the hunter's belt has four close, smaller stars—and a hazy nebula that's easiest to see with binoculars.

The Delta Ponds are flush with ducks. Besides the usual year-round birds—mallards, Canada geese, blue heron, kingfishers, coots and double-crested cormorants—winter visitors have flown in. Old friends are buffleheads, wigeons, northern shovelers, grebes, gadwalls, teal, and ringnecks. Rare in our pond are hooded mergansers and egret. No wood ducks yet.

Hooded mergansers at the Delta Ponds.

Maybe this year I'll be able to photograph a bufflehead. They are incredibly shy and dive as soon as they see me. Buffleheads are definitely diving ducks, not dabbling ducks. If I am lucky enough to train my camera on one, the moment it gets in focus, it dives. Mergansers are better at tolerating observers.

Here's an idea: Give a good pair of binoculars to your loved one for the holidays. If you'd rather look closely at things, give a good triplet hand lens. Magnification reveals the beauty and symmetry of mosses and liverworts. They may all look alike from a distance, but under a hand lens, the tidy rows of liverwort leaves distinguish them from the scruffy spiraled leaves of mosses.

* * *

Sunny mornings are pretty scarce this time of the year, even when days end up sunny. By sunset the the air is filled with moisture. Cool nights and a chilly dawn turn moist air into dense fog in the valley floor. Only after the sun warms the fog banks late in the morning does a sunny day show its predicted blue skies.

Clear days and clear nights are likely to lead to frozen pipes. Thanksgiving brought us our first hard freeze of the season. The nasturtiums went limp overnight. With their cells burst by the freeze, they released a cloud of nasturtium fragrance the next morning.

* * *

Gray whales are headed south this month and most of next month, led by females keen on giving birth in warm lagoons along the coast of Baja California, Mexico. Whale watching is not as good as during the northward migration in spring, when whales move more slowly and closer to shore. But more whales per hour pass Oregon's headlands in winter than in spring, so you're almost guaranteed to see some. It helps to look from a high vantage point, such as Cape Perpetua, Yaquina Head, or Cape Lookout.

* * *

Now is a good time to ponder that a century ago Einstein was polishing up his relativity theories of the cosmos, bracketing the universe from infinitesimally small to unimaginably expansive. Just over a century and a half ago Darwin published the theory of evolution by natural selection. These are the fundamental theories of science that give us our deepest understanding of the real world. Natural history—recording direct observation of nature around us—remains, in my view, at the core of our common science experience.

Even as new subatomic particles are discovered and gravitational waves are detected from across the universe, we can all participate in the practice of science by learning the birds and flowers and passing this knowledge to our children.

* * *

Just like the summer solstice, the winter solstice slips by with hardly a wink or a nod. The approach is so gradual that only a calendar watcher (or a member of a pagan community) knows for sure which day to celebrate.

The turn of the calendar year comes, not coincidentally, at the turn of the solar year. It would be appropriate to celebrate New Year's Day the day after winter solstice. Solstices are milestones in the cycle of nature, not ending and starting points.

Gray fox.

Winter solstice is deeply embedded in spiritual traditions of awakening and renewal. Whether Christmas, Hannukah, Kwanzaa, or Dongzhi, the festivals express a deep appreciation that the sun is the fundamental source of energy for the world we live in. There are mirror winter solstice celebrations in the southern hemisphere. Matakiri of the Maori and Inti Raymi of the Inca occur in our June calendar, similarly marking a new beginning or new cycle coming out of darkness.

The artificial lights and temperature-controlled buildings of our urban culture diminish our understanding of the basic forces of our planetary environment. Our direct connection to the sun has been obscured. The consequences of this disconnect are attacks on our very basis of existence, to the point of denying climate change.

Now, as much as ever, it is important for nature lovers (including nature worshippers) to promote knowledge of the natural world. Knowledge will inspire love of nature and love will inspire positive action. Naturalists, the shamans of an older generation of scientists, have an urgent calling to teach their children, friends, and neighbors. It is both a rewarding and sacred duty, as eighteenth-century poet William Wordsworth wrote, "Knowing that nature never did betray the heart that loved her."

Walk in forests, learn birds, take pictures of flowers and mountains, write letters supporting conservation of natural areas.

Western red cedar cones and leaf scales.

PART TWO

Essays, Observations, and Contemplations

The Three Sisters Wilderness is a place to sit quietly and think.

A Naturalist's Manifesto

One of my favorite places to backpack is Linton Meadows, deep in the Three Sisters Wilderness. It's a place where I feel truly alive, where what I do as a human being is right at the frontier of my consciousness. It's a place where I can sit quietly for hours, listening to the birds and watching the shadows move around the rocks and hummocks of grasses and dwarfy pines. It's a place where I can think about natural history and what it means to be a student of natural history.

The ultimate question for such a student is: What is the future of humanity on this planet? Every ecosystem has a maximum population limit, so our numbers cannot increase forever. The reality is that the earth will survive the maximum human population level and then the population will decline.

What will happen then? Some pursuits will fail. Enjoying life by entertaining ourselves with internal combustion machines has always been limited to a very few and it will be fewer in the future. Playing with motorcycles, power boats, jet skis, snowmobiles, and jeeps are activities too expensive in natural resources to be sustained for long as simple pleasurable pursuits. Humanistic enterprises will increase in strength. The arts will thrive as will spiritual pursuits.

I like to imagine a future where people enjoy just being alive in an environment full of life of all kinds. Walking over the hill and down in the valley, learning the wildflowers, listening to the bird calls, watching the butterflies, tracing the constellations moving across the sky at night, drawing a spider—these are the activities of people filling their lives with natural history.

I've decided that my conservation and teaching efforts should be directed towards maintaining the resources that will provide these future naturalists with the opportunity to enrich their lives. I will strive to protect the untouched forests. I will stop worrying about every new weed that shows up in town. I will do my best to help people enjoy nature, learn to love it, and work to conserve it along with me.

Douglas-fir cone.

Frond Memories of the Tehri Hills

My life's commitment to studying plants began when I was ten years old. My parents were Methodist missionaries in south-central India, close to Hyderabad. I spent most of my time at a boarding school for missionary kids in a town called Mussoorie, in the foothills of the Himalaya Mountains. Woodstock School was at an elevation of 7,000 feet, surrounded by forests teeming with life. My father collected butterflies as a hobby, not unusual for a missionary in the 1940s and 1950s. His interest in natural history must have sparked my passion because I was collecting butterflies by seven or eight.

When I was ten my older brother Stanley was taking biology in high school. His class had been assigned to make a collection of pressed ferns. I was fascinated by the way he and his classmates talked about their search for rare ferns. I found an unusual fern on a big branch while climbing an oak tree and brought it to Stanley. He told me it was a grape fern, one of the rare ferns he had not yet seen. It was a real prize. I put it between the pages of one of the biggest volumes of our Enclycopaedia Brittanica and pressed it.

The following year I was given a chance to make a fern collection as a class project for sixth grade natural science. We were not expected to make as big a collection as the high school biology students but the notion was the same. I could hardly wait for the monsoons to begin, so the rain would revive the ferns.

When monsoon rains arrived in India in late June, butterflies disappeared from the landscape. Beetles came out with the first rains so for a while my attention was on beetle hunting. After a few weeks of good rains, the ferns were ready to collect. When the monsoons ended, the butterflies appeared again, often in a fall brood of different forms. Such was the cycle of activity of the ardent natural history collector. Mussoorie was a wonderful place for a young naturalist.

When I got to high school we had a new biology teacher. I was keen on telling her about the tradition at Woodstock School of having the biology students make a collection of ferns. The standard was a collection of twenty-five different kinds of ferns. I was very happy that she thought this was a good idea. Some of my classmates were not so happy. One day at lunch the girls accused me of lobbying for an unreasonable assignment. So on the way back from our cafeteria to the classroom building, I pointed out seventeen different kinds of ferns growing in the cracks of the rock walls lining the path. My ability and willingness to help with fern collecting had an unexpected side benefit. I garnered respect from girls who previously would just look past me. I wasn't just a geeky nature nut, I had knowledge that was useful. There followed a social feedback that involved my being more attentive to the girls, too. I didn't stop being a geek but I became a popular geek, a role I enjoyed. That year I collected over ninety different kinds of ferns.

Fern study seemed like the pastime for geeks, and it more or less was. But getting the ferns to study was not without adventure and strenuous exercise. Those of us who hunted for ferns often went to places other hikers never thought of going. We slid down steep, forested slopes and slipped over waterfalls to get access to ferny canyons. We climbed vertical cliffs without ropes or pitons. Although often exposed to danger, there was only one time I felt seriously in danger. It was the one time we actually did use a rope.

The most exciting fern I found, when I was sixteen years old, was one that I first spotted from a path across the valley. It was growing at the top of a cliff that rose straight up from a rocky

I eagerly collected ferns in Himalayan canyons.

stream bed. A little scouting showed that the ferns were impossible to approach from my side of the valley. The stream was at monsoon high water, and even if I could cross it, the cliff overhung at the bottom.

Since there was no way to climb up to the ferns, I would have to come down from the other side. I recruited two friends, Dean and Jim, to help me. It was a full-day trip, requiring a fifteen-mile hike each way. With considerable effort, at the end making our way through untracked forest, we finally arrived above the canyon on the side of the stream with the ferns. Dean and Jim planted themselves on the uphill side of a tree just above the cliff. We had brought a rope, little more than a clothes line, which we tied around my waist so they could lower me over the lip of the cliff down to where the ferns were. Such a clever plan!

Theoretically, I would be secured from above while getting to the biggest and best of the ferns. At first this worked beautifully. They lowered me slowly over the cliff. Leaning back against the rope and walking backwards with my body nearly horizontal, I soon had a collecting bag full of ferns. But the top of the cliff wasn't solid rock, it had a lip of soil bound together with roots.

In my swaying back and forth collecting ferns, the rope had cut into the lip that overhung the cliff. I called out to my buddies to pull me up. When they pulled on the rope, it cut deeper into the dirt at the top of the cliff and pinned me underneath the lip. I was stuck! I was like a big button trying to get through a buttonhole that was too small. I yelled at them to stop, slack off, and release me.

What to do? The rope wasn't long enough for them to lower me to the bottom of the cliff. And in any case, we had no idea if I could get out of the canyon—if I didn't drown. The rope was cutting into their hands, and it was cutting me in half. This was a time for desperation. I planted my feet on the cliff face and with both hands jerked the rope a little bit out of the slot it had cut. Dean and Jim pulled me up just a bit. We did that over and over again. Meanwhile, Jim and Dean felt the whole hillside start to slide under them, anchor tree and all. The ground was moving like a glacier over bedrock. They were as scared as I was of falling into the stream.

I can't remember exactly how I got up because I didn't spare any energy to think. I just kept gasping and trying to keep my hands from getting jammed in the slot under the taut rope. Finally I was able to reach over the lip and grasp the rope above where it had sawn the groove. A little more heaving and puffing and Dean could grab my arm and pull me to safety.

We had scored the only record of *Drynaria propinqua* from the Tehri Hills. And it was that experience of discovering something new that led me into botany. In all my years in India, until graduating from high school, I never caught a butterfly the British hadn't reported before me. My explorations for ferns, on the other hand, regularly turned up specimens that nobody in the area had found before. A few of my specimens might even have been new to science. The thrill of discovery set me on my life's path.

A Tour of the Solar System

My wife Connie and I joined a flock of other bicyclists for a fundraising bike ride dedicated to the care of the solar system model along the bike path by the Willamette River in Eugene. As a fundraiser the trip was a huge success. As a natural history educational tour, it was less successful because everybody was so keen on just cycling away in the glorious sunshine that our guide, model maker Jack Van Dusen, had little chance to talk about the object of our attention. One highlight of the day was learning a great mnemonic sentence for remembering the planets in order, invented by a young girl the night before: "My very energetic mother just showed us nine planets."

Eugene's solar system model is built to a scale of one to one billion. There are very few cities with similar models, two in Europe and a smaller one in Denver. Ours is centered in Alton Baker Park where a large, yellow sphere, about four and a half feet in diameter, is located next to the pond at the north end of the DeFazio Bike Bridge. Pluto, the outermost planet-cum-dwarf planet, is located 3.67 miles away in the shadow of the Beltline bridge. Jack considered putting the closest star into this model but the earth isn't big enough. Alpha Centauri would have to be 37,000 miles away, and it's only about 25,000 miles around the earth.

The innermost planets of the solar system model are located near Alton Baker Park's pond. Mercury is to the east, barely far enough away to make it worth mounting your bicycle for a ride. In the scale of the model, Mercury is smaller than a pea; it looks like a red BB mounted on a slender pyramid. At this scale Mercury would take nine minutes to move one inch in its orbit of the sun.

A full moon on the summer solstice.

The Earth and the moon are another hundred yards in the same direction. Standing next to Earth and looking back at the sun, it is easy to understand why Mercury and Venus are seen at certain times of the year, and only in the morning or evening at that. Because their orbit is inside of Earth's, most of the time they are either behind the sun or in front of the sun. They are seen only when they are off to the side of the sun, but never far off, so they can be seen only in morning or evening. Having this explained to you isn't always easy to grasp, but walking around the model makes this kind of celestial phenomenon understandable through direct experience.

Venus and Mars are on the far side of the pond from the sun to emphasize that the solar system really is spread out in space. From here on out the planets are abnormally lined up, but that was the only way Jack could keep the model along a reasonable bike path in the city parks. As we traversed outward, we were given reminders of this by comments such as, "Saturn could have been placed among the science buildings on the University of Oregon campus," "Uranus could have been on the Lane Community College campus," and "Neptune could be in Island Park in Springfield."

When we took our tour Jupiter was missing, as was Neptune. Our fundraiser was part of the effort to help replace the missing planets. The challenge is to find a way to anchor the planets more securely so that vandals can't rip them off. It's funny how many times Pluto has been reported stolen. The truth is that Pluto is so small that its site appears to have just a pedestal with nothing on top at all.

We can be very grateful to Jack Van Dusen and his son, who was the one with the original inspiration to create this model. Carl Sagan once said that a view from space is what it takes to develop a suitable perspective of our importance on this planet. With Lane County's solar system model, we can directly experience that perspective.

Venus and Jupiter sharing a July evening sky.

Winter, the Season of My Content

As autumn moves into its final weeks, we look forward to what people around here laughingly call winter. Ah, winter! Too often the notion of winter conjures up a season of hibernation and dormancy. My dictionary suggests winter is ". . . a period of decline, decay, inertia, dreariness, or adversity." How wrong this is for us here in the Willamette Valley of western Oregon! We have merely entered the rainy season, the long, wet season that connects fall with spring. Only in the occasional years when snow falls can we claim a moment of winter here in the valley.

The onset of the rainy season brings on a new life to the woodlands and fields. It is true that deciduous trees like oaks and maples, and most of the woody shrubs, drop their leaves and enter dormancy, but most of the native plants spring to life in the "winter" and actually have their primary dormant period in the drought of the summer. The mosses and lichens are entering their main season of growth and reproduction. Perennial herbs start stirring, charging their leaf primordia to burst above ground with burgeoning foliage. They appear prominently around Christmas. Watch for the tall larkspur, cow parsnip, and poison hemlock to be the first really big leaves to come up.

Then there are the winter annuals. I love to watch them grow. These are plants that germinate with the coming of the fall rains and grow all winter. They are among the first to bloom in the new year, long before most people can think of spring. Most will set seed before you get your garden well started. The exotic western bittercress is as successful a weed as anything in your garden. In early spring it will be the farthest along, too. Bittercress will already have a half-dozen leaves when most garden sprouts have only one or two.

Meadowrue's leaves uncurl as a green bouquet.

I made a series of silhouettes to help folks identify the common seedlings they see when out for a walk. Seedling identification is a little trickier than flower identification, a winter challenge. Almost all of the early sprouters have two cotyledons—the seed leaves that give the name dicotyledon to a major group of flowering plants. It's interesting that for most of these the cotyledons are very different from the typical "mature" leaves of the plants. Only the chickweed has cotyledons like the mature ones. My favorite is the humble, overlooked bedstraw. It has two huge cotyledons that are bigger than any of the leaflets of the plant until it gets around to putting on summer leaves.

Why I Like Mosses

People who know me and who have gone on my winter plant walks have heard me go on and on about mosses. I love mosses. I also love liverworts. These are the fluffy green plants that put a shag on the trunks and drape from the branches of trees in the Pacific Northwest. I like the lichens, too, the plant-like things that put a colorful crust on the bark and give the oak and ash branch tips their gray-green cast in the rainy season.

I like mosses not merely because of how they look. They are pretty enough, of course, especially if you use a lens or microscope. I like mosses and their ilk because of what they do. There are two special things about them that impress me more than anything. One is how they deal with the dry season and the second is how they deal with the rainy season.

In a normal year, our area has a six-week dry period at the end of summer with very little rain. But the dry season keeps getting longer. By fall the mosses, liverworts, and lichens in Lane County are just as crispy as could be.

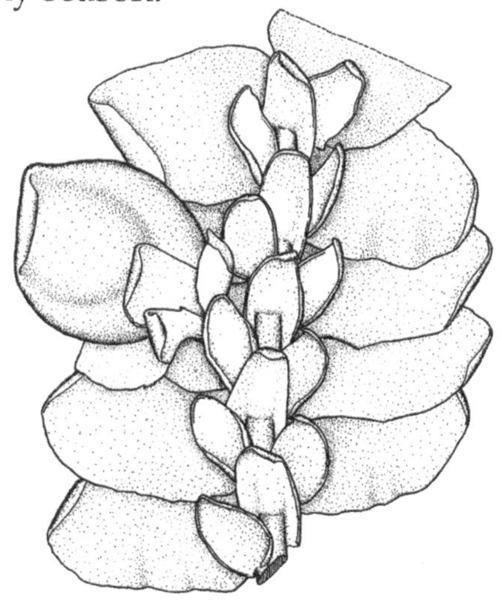

Like most epiphytic liverworts, the tree ruffle liverwort can survive desiccation.

These plants are epiphytes, not parasites. Epiphyte means "upon the plant." Mosses perch on the branches, attaching themselves to the bark without penetrating to the conducting system of the trees. This is a

After a drought, rain brings mosses like this Oregon feather moss back to life.

desiccating habitat, just like a bare rock face. It dries things out very rapidly. One researcher said that a moss growing on bare rock in the sun is drier, on a percent moisture basis, than the USDA specifications for flour on a grocery store shelf. Dry but alive. Mosses and liverworts (and lichens) on the oak and ash branches are both dry and alive. They are desiccation tolerant. Most flowering plants and conifers are not desiccation tolerant. Things like cacti and succulents are desiccation resistant, meaning that they store water extremely well, so they can last through a drought without completely drying. But if they actually dried out so their tissues were as dry as a moss on an oak tree, they would die. Only about twenty kinds of flowering plants are truly desiccation tolerant.

According to a recent review of the phenomenon, desiccation tolerance was a characteristic of the very first land plants. These appeared in earth's history around 500 million years ago. As plants evolved internal water conducting systems they lost the ability to survive desiccation. Apparently this is because tissue that retains moisture is more efficient at growing. The few flowering plants that have evolved (or reverted back to) desiccation tolerance have done it at least eight different times. It's never been a very popular way to go.

Unlike mosses, liverworts are closely related to the first land plants. All this time, they have retained their ability to survive drying out. This desiccation tolerance is what allows liverworts to occupy micro habitats that the "higher" plants ignore: on open rock surfaces and on branches of trees in climates with frequent, long dry spells.

What's amazing about desiccation tolerant mosses is that they can start their life processes in a very few minutes after they are rehydrated. Almost as soon as their cells absorb water, they start making food. They combine carbon dioxide from the atmosphere with the water and, using energy from the sun, synthesize sugars. This is photosynthesis, the process of life that gives energy to all living things. In most higher plants the enzymes that do photosynthesis disintegrate when the cells dry out. These desiccation intolerant plants die when they dry. And this is why desiccation tolerance is so wonderful. Somehow, mosses are able to protect the photosynthetic enzymes in their cells from disintegrating. They're ready to go to work immediately upon rehydration. The cells don't have to make new enzymes.

Nobody has yet figured out how mosses do this. There's exciting work to be done in this area. Look for the genetic engineers of the next generation to unlock the secrets of the mosses and put the genes for desiccation tolerance into crop plants. They will be valuable in the drier parts of the earth. Imagine an annual crop that you don't have to water; just plant and wait for the rain. After the soil dries out again, the plants merely shrivel and go dormant instead of drying and dying. With the next rain they'll spring to life again and grow further until that dose of water is used, and so on until ready for harvest.

What is a fantasy for genetic engineers is a part of everyday

Lepidozia reptans, *the dozing reptile liverwort.*

life for the mosses on the oaks around us. Step outside and give them another look. Gives you a new respect for them, doesn't it?

Everyone knows that mosses like wet weather. The rainy season is when mosses are the most prominent and are growing the fastest. Because mosses on the branches of trees are not parasitic, they cannot get moisture from the host trees, nor can they get essential nutrients from the host trees. Where then do mosses get their food and water?

Some essential elements are easy to get, like carbon from carbon dioxide in the atmosphere. Many others are quite scarce in the environment, especially metals which need to be absorbed as ions of dissolved metallic salts. Mosses must obtain all the elements necessary for growth from the only source available, the air around them. A certain amount is blown in as dust during dry weather and made available when the dust is wetted by the rain. But the nutrient elements present in dust are just as likely to be washed away by the rain as absorbed by the mosses' plant tissue. Furthermore, there's not likely to be an adequate supply of essential elements in dust. So where in air do mosses get their nutrients? From the rain! The rain that comes from the air around them.

Rain water does not have a lot of dissolved elements in it but it always has some. What is special about mosses is that their cell walls have a special affinity for the dissolved elements. Moss cells use a process called ion exchange to get rare elements in ionic form. Moss cells are able to scavenge essential elements from the most dilute of solutions, even rain water. Any nutrients in the dust on the mosses are also snapped up if they are wetted by rain. In this way mosses get what they need—not very much, just enough to grow slowly. Slow growing seems to be just fine for mosses.

This ability to scavenge elements from dilute solutions is much better developed in mosses than in flowering plants. That's why mosses do so well in your lawn during the winter. That's why mosses, not grasses, grow on your roof. The winter rains wash away all the nutrients that grasses need to grow, but provide enough for the mosses to thrive. This special ability to scavenge elements is used against mosses in the Moss Kill formulations people use to eliminate mosses from lawns and roofs. The Moss Kill compounds rely on salts of metals like zinc and copper. Zinc and copper are actually essential elements for mosses. The special ion exchange capacity of moss cell walls pulls out the copper and zinc ions they need from rain water. When there is an excess of these metals, however, too much is pulled into moss cells. Too much copper or zinc in moss cells poisons them. Even slightly elevated levels of zinc and copper, harmless to most flowering plants, are toxic to mosses. Alas, the zinc that runs off from treated roofs and lawns turns out to also be toxic to fish, and has contributed to the decline of salmon throughout the Pacific Northwest.

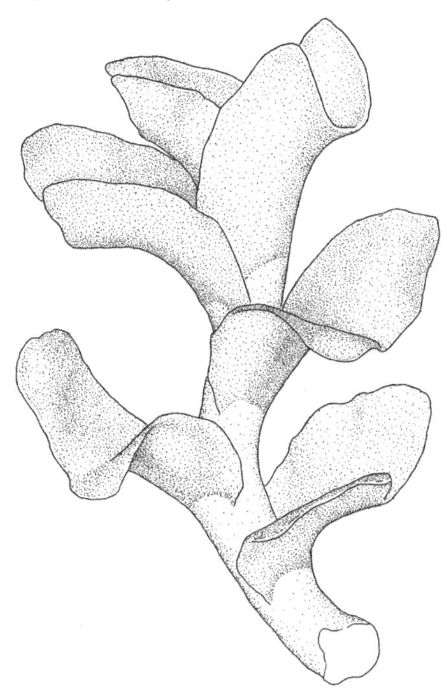

Scapania obscura, the shy ladderwort.

The use of copper or zinc to poison mosses demonstrates that the ion exchange capacity of mosses could yet be put to

*Mosses like this opalescent moss (*Pohlia cruda*) may be extremely small, but they play an important role in the ecosystem.*

economic advantage. Surprisingly, hardly anybody mentions that this special ability of mosses might be extremely important to one of our most prominent ecosystems. I refer to the rain forests found along the Pacific Coast from northern California to Alaska.

The rain forests of the Pacific Coast are characterized by the abundance of mosses festooning the branches of every tree and shrub as well as carpeting every open square foot of forest floor. The mosses are what tell you this is a rain forest. So, are the mosses just there for decoration? Are they there just to take advantage of the situation, because they can grow in rainy forests better than in the inland forests? I think most ecologists have been satisfied to accept this explanation. What they are overlooking is that mosses are an essential element of the rain forests, that the rain forests would not be the forests they are without the mosses.

It's all about the rain. Rain washes away the dissolved nutrients in the soil, away from the roots of the trees and flowers. Only the mosses are able to capture the essential elements from the rain water and fix them into biological compounds available for all plants of the ecosystem. That's my theory anyway. You read it here first. Mosses are responsible for the nutrient health of our rain forest ecosystems. And that is why I like mosses.

Talking Stones

The Kalapuya Talking Stones were dedicated in the Whilamut Natural Area of Alton Baker Park in 2003. This natural area takes up most of the park east of Eugene's Leisure Lane, where the park host is located, and continues under the I-5 freeway to the western edge of Springfield. The name Whilamut, comes from a Kalapuyan word meaning "where the river ripples and runs fast," and is the origin of the Willamette river's name.

Scattered throughout the natural area are eleven large rocks deeply etched with words from the Kalapuya language. These are the Kalapuya Talking Stones. The words were chosen to reflect various features of the natural area with the rocks placed appropriately. The rock with the word "Whilamut" is placed alone, next to the river, nearly in the center of the natural area. Next to the rock there is a bench where one can sit and reflect on the history of the area.

The Eugene Natural History Society has been involved with this natural area for a long time, going back to when it was a county park. The ENHS was instrumental in getting the county to designate a portion of Alton Baker Park as a natural area, but this designation was lost when the park was turned over to the city. A citizen planning committee worked with the parks' departments of both Eugene and Springfield to enlarge and re-establish the natural area. As the talking stones were being installed, we began a discussion with the planners and designers about the idea of "seeding" the talking stones with moss so their appearance might seem more settled, that they had been there for a long time and really belonged. After getting a nod from all involved, the project began.

The first inoculation of the stones took place on a nature walk I led on an October Sunday. Participants in this event included Dave Sonnichsen of the Citizen Planning Committee and Lisa Ponder, the artist who designed and directed the installation of the stones. On that day we painted five of the eleven stones with a slurry of buttermilk, egg, and moss. The slurry was made by pouring a pint of buttermilk into a blender and dropping in mosses a pinch at a time. The mosses were fragmented on the "puree" speed until the machine could take no more. In the end, about an equal volume of dry moss and buttermilk were mixed, followed by the addition of one large egg to act as a sticking agent. Then, with the aid of a paint brush, we dabbed on the slurry, tucking it into the corners and crevices of the stones.

The moss species we used are typical for rocks in both sun and shade. A mix was important because some of the talking stones are in the shade and some in full sun. The most prominent species in the moss inoculum are *Racomitrium elongatum, Racomitrium varium, Grimmia trichophylla, Tortula princeps, Ceratodon purpureus,* and *Homalothecium pinnatifidum.*

The mosses for the first batch were collected from roadside rocks near Gillespie Butte. The second batch was made with mosses gathered from an abandoned quarry on Mt. Pisgah, where the rocks closely match the talking stones. Because the first slurry contained some rather large chunks of moss, the second batch was done differently. The dried moss was fragmented in a coffee grinder until it was about the size of an espresso grind. A cup of the ground moss was added to a pint of buttermilk and two large eggs were mixed in. This slurry seemed to behave much better, even sticking to vertical surfaces, as we painted it onto the stones in the eastern part of the natural area on the last day of October. Future springs will show whether the fragments regenerate into new plants as hoped.

Thirty Years of Years

This year marks the sesquicentennial of one of the most famous criminal trials in U.S. history, when Abraham Lincoln defended a man against murder charges with the aid of an almanac. The star witness of the "Almanac Trial" in 1858 claimed he saw the defendant bashing in a man's head by the light of a three-quarters moon high in the sky. Lincoln led the witness to emphasize how bright the moonlight was, that it was a critical element of his certitude. Then Lincoln pulled out an Old Farmer's Almanac and showed the court that at the time the witness claimed to see the assault, the moon was barely above the horizon. There was no bright moon high in the sky. The defendant was acquitted. Although there was other supporting evidence in Lincoln's favor, this is the part of the story that most people have heard.

This story has a special place in my heart. I've been producing a Willamette Valley Nature Calendar for more than thirty years. My calendar is really an almanac because it does more than depict the days of the week for each month and assign holidays. It includes the phases of the moon, like many calendars on the market, but it also has gardening tips and a compendium of natural events to be expected throughout the year.

I've learned many things about calendar making over the years. I had never noticed, for example, that the sunrise and sunset times are not symmetrical around the solstices. As the winter solstice approaches, sunrise keeps getting later and sunset earlier until the shortest day of the year is reached. However, the earliest sunset occurs several weeks before the solstice and the latest sunrise a similar period after the solstice. The times are like two curves that are out of phase. The shortest day represents the point where the curves are closest. I have not been able to find a clear explanation for this. My best guess is that it has to do with the fact that that sunrise occurs on the side of the earth that is moving in the direction of the earth's orbit and sunset on the side moving opposite the direction of orbit. Visualizing this is a terrific mental exercise.

Much of my pleasure in making these calendars has come from the research for the nature notes. I've enjoyed contributions of people like Herb Wisner, who shared his knowledge of when

I made the first nature calendar in 1979. Notes were typewritten, no drawings.

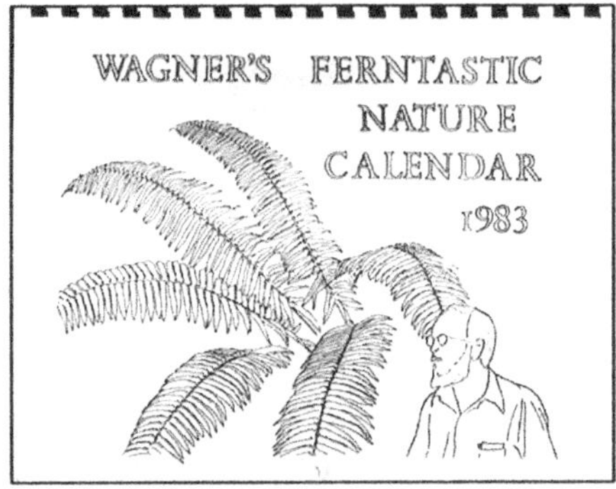

1982 marked the beginning of continuous production, with drawings of ferns and liverworts featured.

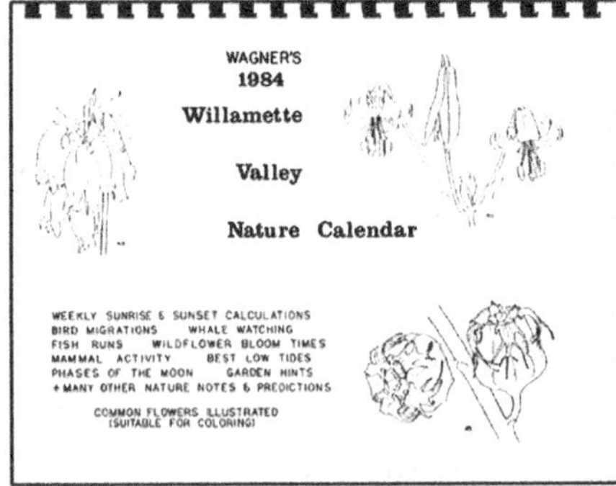

The title, "Wagner's Willamette Valley Nature Calendar" first appeared on the 1984 calendar.

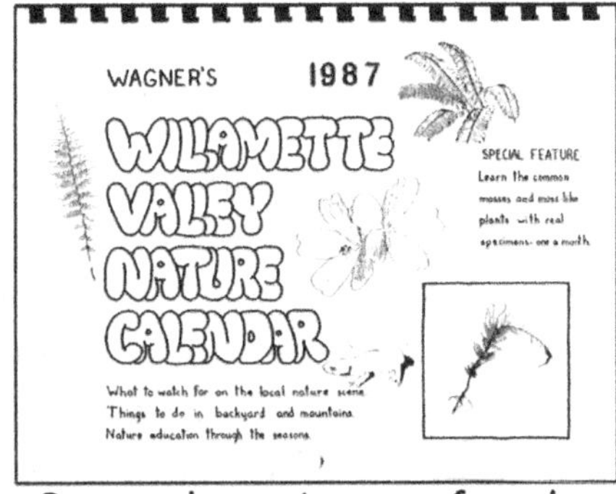

Pressed specimens of real plants were pasted into every calendar. This year is a real collector's item.

bird migrations take place, and the late Leighton Ho, whose love of fishing gave me the information on most fish runs. Many of the observations are just that, personal observations made over the years. Most important were the weekly plant walks that I led in Alton Baker Park each spring for seventeen years.

Calendar making could be a boring enterprise if all one were doing was laying out dates for the days of the week. There are only seven possibilities: years that begin on Sunday, on Monday, and so on until Saturday. Leap years cause a minor problem because you have to use months from two different years. I try to

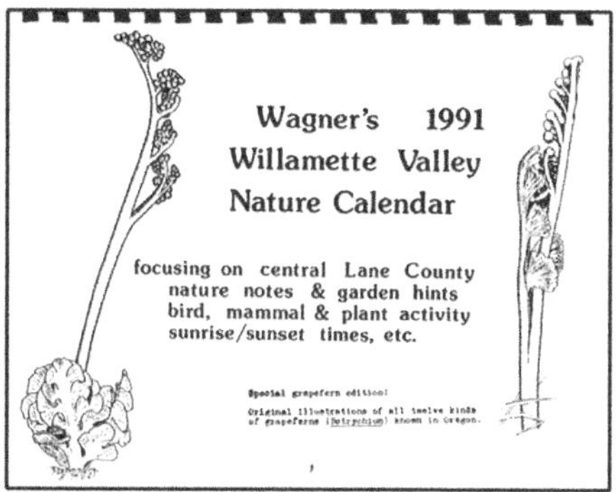

1991 featured drawings of every species of moonwort and grapefern known to grow in Oregon: exactly twelve.

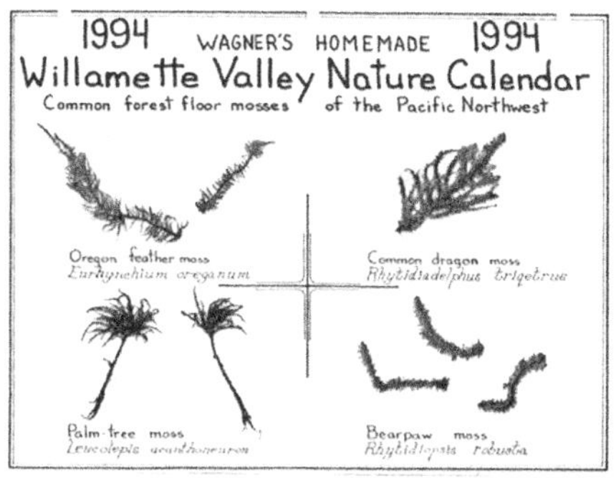

In the fall of 1993 another calendar was made with pressed moss specimens pasted onto every one.

The last experiment with illustrations that were not drawings, the 2000 calendar had photographs instead.

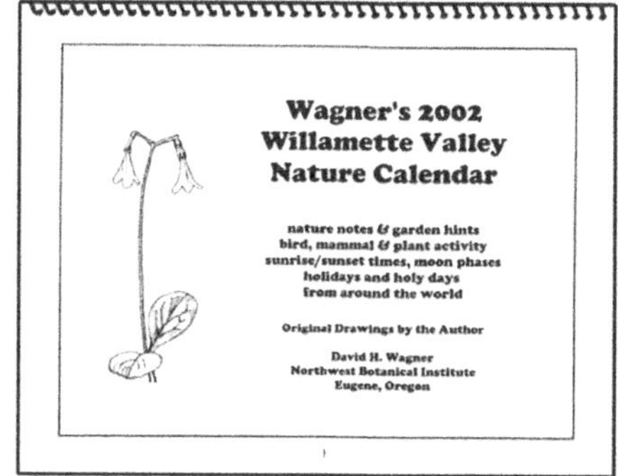

Spiral bindings appeared with the 2002 calendar. Since then all have featured detailed pen and ink stipple drawings.

keep things interesting by making each calendar a little bit different. Some things are worth noting each year – for example, when do newts move downhill to breed in valley ponds? We always want to know that. One year I learned that our great horned owls begin nesting in January. That's definitely news for a calendar.

The other thing I try to make different each year is the monthly illustration. Thanks to spousal urging, I've put more and more effort into the drawings. The subject matter has expanded over the recent years also. As a botanist, my illustrations in early years were almost all of flowers. It has been an invigorating challenge to draw insects, herps, birds, and mammals. As I said to a friend recently, "the attitude of turtles is so different from orchids."

Later calendar illustrations were arduously stippled, shaded with tiny dots, as for this rough-skinned newt.

New Zealand

My wife and I spent a little over two weeks driving around and exploring the fascinating country of New Zealand. We toured the South Island, which is about the same latitude south as Oregon is north. One of the things that struck us was how much of what we saw was familiar. And most of that which was familiar didn't really belong!

New Zealand was settled by Europeans relatively recently, in the last century and a half. Much as in our own country, that contact permanently altered the landscape. All the beautiful, pastoral scenes with sheep were originally covered with dense forests. The only extensive wild areas that remain are along the west coast, where the rain forests have never been amenable to clearing and settlement.

When we walked along the trails, I saw one of my old friends from our home garden: the weedy liverwort, *Lunularia cruciata*. This liverwort is not native to Oregon. It was introduced here from Europe. Just as it is now growing all over Eugene, it is now growing in almost every place we stopped in New Zealand. It was along the paths in every Scenic Reserve and every National Park walkway.

In the gardens and along roadsides were lots of temperate weeds that gave an eerie sense of familiarity. They were familiar, but they didn't belong. Although the New Zealanders claim to love their flora, their gardens have as few native plants as those in our neighborhood. Roses from England are as popular there as they are here. Petunias and begonias are equally prominent.

The most common birds in the towns are starlings, followed

by house sparrows. The native birds are mostly shy forest creatures, except for the fantail, which is the friendliest wild bird I've ever encountered. As with many islands, New Zealand has lost many native birds, especially the ground-nesting ones, because there were not any native predators. Introduced rats and weasel-like stoats have taken a deadly toll.

*The crescent-cup liverwort (*Lunularia cruciata*) is native to Europe and is common in Oregon, but is an invasive weed in New Zealand.*

In fact, New Zealand has only three native mammals—three species of bats, and one is already extinct. All other mammals are introduced. Red deer and mountain goats from the Himalayas became so common in the mountains that professional hunters were hired to reduce their numbers. Now they are trapped and raised on farms.

The most curious introduction of all is the possum. The animal referred to here is not the American opossum but a marsupial native to Australia. It was introduced in the late 1800s to supply the fur trade. When the fur market declined in the 1980s, this animal proliferated dramatically to the extent that it has become a serious threat to the native forests. Possums eat over 20,000 tons of leafy material every night. Large expanses of forest have been denuded. The possums' abundance is demonstrated by road kill. One morning we counted over fifty along the roadside, more than one every two miles. It is a striking example that what is common or familiar in New Zealand may be as much a stranger as the visitor.

The Value of Natural History

I love natural history because I enjoy being outdoors and I find nature fascinating. But there are also some practical benefits that come from the study of natural history. Knowing a few constellations once got me out of a dangerous and awkward situation.

The story dates to my first summer of teaching. I was working in Seattle, at the University of Washington, teaching their summer plant taxonomy class. This was a very big class with several dozen students. Gathering material for their labs had me spending entire weekends exploring the Cascade Mountains for good specimens. I would camp out in a state van filled with ice chests for storing flower specimens.

One weekend I was in the high, rounded, hill country near Lake Chelan. As evening drew near, I parked on the top of a ridge. It was a beautiful spot with a view for miles all around. I ate my dinner of a few sandwiches and sat in the cab enjoying the sight. Waiting for darkness to fall before getting into my sleeping bag, I noticed a rock outcrop about fifty yards along the ridge and wondered if there were any interesting ferns growing on it. There was still plenty of light left, so I decided to check it out. I strolled up to the outcrop and looked it over. There was nothing of note, but I saw there was another rock outcrop less than a hundred yards farther along the ridge. "Aha," I said to myself, "there's plenty of time to get up there and back to the van before it gets too dark to see my way." So I took off up the ridge to this second rocky knoll. As I walked along, I didn't notice that the cloud layer had started dropping.

The weather had been reasonably good throughout the day,

not sunny but pleasant enough below a layer of high clouds. My eyes were on the rock and the crevices that might have ferns in them. I had barely gotten to the outcrop when wisps of fog started blowing around me. "Oops," I said to myself, "I'd better get back to the van. I don't have a flashlight or even a jacket. The mist is going to make it hard to see where I'm going. But all I have to do is stay right on the crest of the ridge."

And so I took off at a brisk pace, headed back to the van. Before taking fifty steps, I came to a fence. "Hmmm," I said to myself, "I didn't go through any fences when I came up here. I must be headed the wrong way. I'd better go back to the top of the ridge where the van is." I corrected my direction and took off again, as briskly as I could in the thickening mist. It was getting dark fast. And then I came to another fence. "Rats!" I said to myself. This meant that I was quite unsure of the correct direction to walk to get to the cozy shelter of the van.

To keep experimenting with different directions could be very dangerous. The roundness of the top of the ridge meant it would be all too easy to go on a spur ridge without knowing I wasn't on the main ridge top. The only sensible thing to do was stay right where I was until I could determine the right way back to the van. And staying right there, as long as it was dark and foggy, meant having to spend a night in the unprotected cold. It started to drizzle. This was not going to be fun. I went back a few steps to a small rock cliff I'd passed and crept under an overhang. It was a small cliff that didn't offer much protection. I tried to build a fire, scavenging the smallest, driest twigs I could find. They were damp so I needed a fire starter. I pulled out my wallet and searched through it for pieces of paper I thought were expendable. Only a couple of scraps were available and they quickly burned away without getting the twigs ignited. So I just huddled up against the rock cliff, trying to get as comfortable as possible while keeping my back to the wind and rain. I was right; it was not fun. I shivered and maybe even dozed for an hour or two.

Suddenly I looked up and rejoiced. The clouds were getting thin as the wind blew them apart. I jumped to my feet and

When the clouds cleared I spotted the North Star between the big dipper and Cassiopeia, and I knew which direction to go.

searched the sky. I found what I was looking for: the Big Dipper. Right off the end of the dipper is the North Star, which meant that my van would be down the ridge in a certain direction. Less than five minutes later I was safely back in the van, nestled in my sleeping bag, soundly and happily asleep.

The lessons of this story are many. Most revolve around how stupid it is to leave your camp late in the evening without a jacket, a compass or emergency gear. It demonstrates how quickly an experienced outdoorsman can get turned around, not really lost but forced to spend a night in the open because of inattention. The happy lesson is how valuable it was for me to know how to recognize the constellation that gave me my bearings. If I hadn't known how to find the North Star, I would have spent the whole night in misery.

What's in a Name?

I have been asked on a number of occasions to give an opinion regarding the correct scientific name for the state flower of Oregon, the Oregon grape. Some sources list it as *Berberis aquifolium* and others as *Mahonia aquifolium*.

With *Berberis* vs. *Mahonia*, what name one uses depends on the purpose for the name. If what's needed is something that reflects current biological thinking, use *Berberis*. If you need something that people think of when gardening, and they don't give a hoot about biology, then use *Mahonia*. Botanists recognize that what is called *Mahonia* refers to a group of plants that fall within the bounds of a natural group that must be called *Berberis* (based on the priority rule of botanical nomenclature). Horticulturists will persist in using the name *Mahonia* because it describes a particular ornamental regardless of biological relationships.

The situation is similar to that with frogs versus toads, rhododendrons versus azaleas, and birds versus reptiles. When people know only a few representatives of large groups, they like to try to divide them into two big, neat piles. However, when detailed studies of these groups are done, it is sometimes found that the situation is more complicated.

There is no natural division between frogs and toads. Instead, there are many groups of tailless amphibians. Some of the things that people want to call frogs are more closely related to toads. As one herpetologist told me, all toads are frogs but not all frogs are toads. It would be better from a biological standpoint to call them all aneurans and not use the term toad or frog at all.

Rhododendron and *Azalea* are not natural genera. Even horticulturalists now appreciate that there are several groups in the genus *Rhododendron* that combine various traits of what were traditionally used to distinguish *Rhododendron* from *Azalea*. So we now keep all of them in a large genus *Rhododendron*—botanically, that is. In popular language we still talk of an azalea (deciduous, usually five stamens) as a different kind of plant than a rhododendron (evergreen, usually ten stamens). This difference means something to a landscape designer that satisfies a need to describe a particular type of garden element.

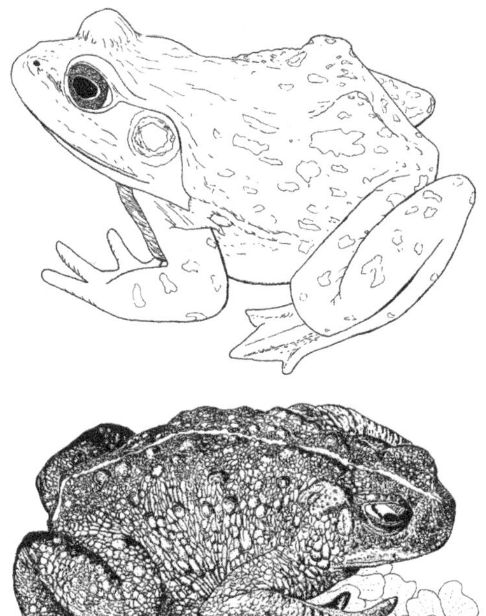

There is no natural natural division between frogs (above) and toads (below).

The same thing is true of birds and reptiles, although this distinction is perhaps the hardest to accept. The fossil record makes clear that there is a group of reptiles that includes the birds and then there are other groups of reptiles that are less related to the bird-like ones. So strong is the historical, intuitive sensibility, that in popular usage people will continue to separate birds and reptiles even though birds are, from a biological standpoint, a group of feathered reptiles related to dinosaurs. Crocodiles and most dinosaurs are more closely related to birds than they are to snakes or turtles.

There is no such thing as an Official International Registry of Botanical Names. The International Code of Botanical Nomenclature tells one how to use a name and how to determine if it is valid when used in a particular way. Coming up with what name to use is left up to the scientist or name user. This is called taxonomic decision. So long as the name follows the rules of nomenclature, it can be considered correct. If I want to treat the monotropoids (candy stripe, pine drops, Indian pipe, etc.) as a separate family, *Monotropaceae,* that's my taxonomic call. *Monotropaceae* is an accepted, valid name. Somebody else is just as correct (nomenclaturally and biologically) to say the monotropoids represent a subfamily of the *Ericaceae* and call them by a subfamily name, *Monotropoideae.* As my taxonomy professor, Marion Ownbey, used to say, "There is no objective means of determining rank in a hierarchy."

However, remember what Ralph Waldo Emerson said: "A foolish consistency is the hobgoblin of a small mind." The purpose of names is for our convenience. Naming is not science. It is nice when names reflect current biological thinking, but there will be no consensus because our system of naming doesn't exactly match evolutionary processes.

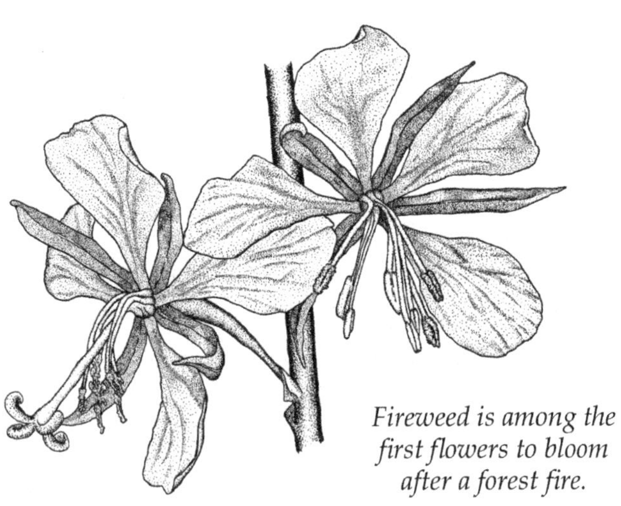

Fireweed is among the first flowers to bloom after a forest fire.

Some trees are more prone to skeletonization than others. The most commonly found ones are those of the Oregon ash. Anywhere ash leaves have lain untouched all winter is a likely spot to find leaf skeletons. I've found that blueberries produce leaf skeletons almost as readily and just as beautiful. My favorites are the leaves of the vanillaleaf (*Achlys*). It's necessary to go up to the mountains to find it, and now is the time. The leaf skeletons are fragile. If you wait until the spring flush of foliage emerges from the ground, it will be too late. The emerging grass and other stems quickly grow through the tender skeins and it is impossible to extract them after this happens. Further decomposition takes its toll too.

I have been keeping a collection of skeletonized leaves. I'm always on the lookout for ones that do not get skeletonized so often. Alder leaves usually decompose rapidly and completely. I was lucky to find one that had lost some of the fine structure but it made for a nice image to reproduce.

Searching for and gathering skeletonized leaves can add a new dimension to the way we walk in the woods. The leaf skeletons usually dry quickly in a few folds of newspaper put under a brick or board. I like to keep them in transparent picture pages such as used for photographs so I can hold them up to the light and see the patterns. It's yet another way to enjoy the miracles of nature.

The First Blooms of Spring

It is not often that I see the goldthread, *Coptis laciniata,* in bloom. On a Saturday in early March I led a group of botanists along the lower Brice Creek Trail in the Cottage Grove District of the Umpqua National Forest. Many patches of *Coptis* were just coming into bloom. Seeing these delicate flowers at the beginning of their bloom period made me think about other early bloomers I've seen in spring.

Each year our first blooms are coming earlier. In town I saw both spring beauty *(Cardamine nuttallii)* and osoberry ("Indian plum" or *Oemleria cerasiformis*) fully in bloom on the last day of January. The normal date for both of these around Eugene has traditionally been February 15. The average date has gradually been moving up because of global warming.

A landmark article in *Nature,* one of the most prestigious international science journals, suggested that global warming is advancing spring events by 2.3 days per decade. The study included comparative analyses of over 1,700 species. The article suggested that at our latitude the shift is actually closer to 4.2 days earlier per decade. This means that since I started making observations of first bloom in spring of 1977, the average first bloom times can now be expected to be from about five to ten days earlier.

So let's look at what blooms when in Lane County. The following plants were observed during the first years of the UO Herbarium spring plant walks, beginning in 1977. The number at left refers to the week of the walk, with 1.00 denoting the first week of March, and 9.00 denoting the ninth week after the first

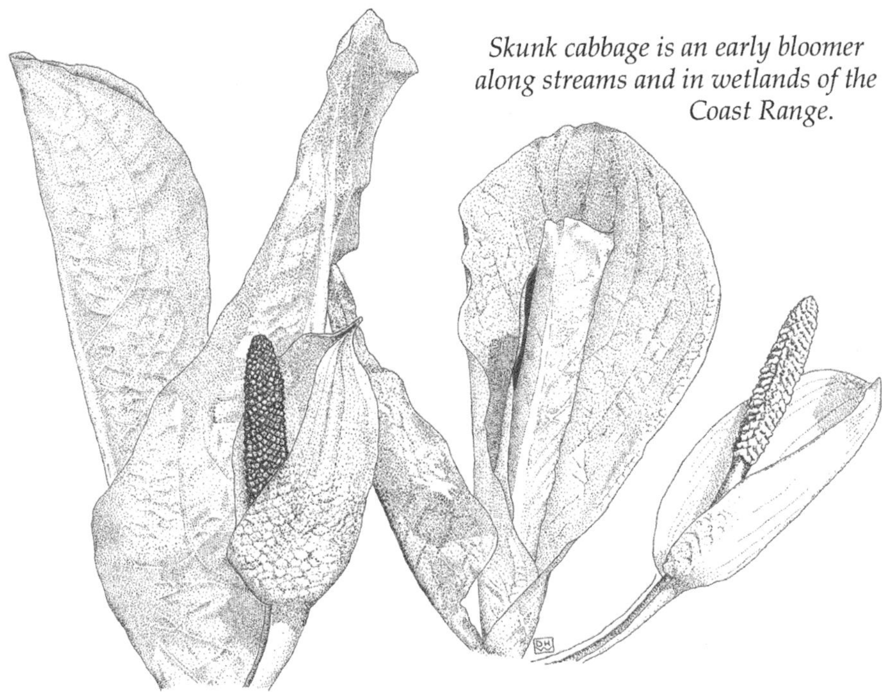

Skunk cabbage is an early bloomer along streams and in wetlands of the Coast Range.

week in March. A score of 3.60 for the blood currant, for example, means that average time of first bloom for *Ribes sanguineum* was between the third and fourth week of March. The number of years each was observed is also given. These results are from the first twelve years of the walks, from 1977 to 1988. The number after the name, on the right, shows how many of those twelve years the plant in question was observed.

MARCH

1.00 *Alnus rhombifolia,* white alder 3
1.00 *Cardamine oligosperma,* western little bittercress 12
1.17 *Cardamine nuttallii,* spring beauty 12
1.17 *Oemleria cerasiformis,* osoberry, Indian plum 12
1.17 *Populus trichocarpa,* black cottonwood 12
1.42 *Draba verna,* spring whitlowgrass 12
1.73 Berberis *aquifolium*, Oregon grape 11
2.57 *Salix sitchensis,* Sitka willow 7
3.33 *Alnus rubra,* red alder 6

3.58 *Nemophila parviflora,* small-flower grovelover 12
3.60 *Ribes sanguineum,* blood currant 5
3.83 *Acer macrophyllum,* bigleaf maple 12
4.00 *Erythronium oregonum,* fawn lily 1
4.00 *Ranunculus occidentalis,* western buttercup 1
5.17 *Ribes divaricatum,* straggly gooseberry 6
5.18 *Rubus ursinus,* Pacific dewberry 11
5.33 *Claytonia perfoliata,* common miner's lettuce 12

APRIL

5.50 *Dicentra formosa,* bleeding heart 12
5.58 *Maianthemum racemosum,* big smilacina, solomonseal 12
5.83 *Tellima grandiflora,* fringecup 12
5.89 *Calandrinia ciliata,* redmaids 9
6.00 *Carex aquatilis,* water sedge 1
6.00 *Salix lucida lasiandra,* Pacific willow 1
6.18 *Lupinus micranthus,* field lupine 11
6.33 *Delphinium trolliifolium,* tall larkspur 12
6.50 *Amelanchier alnifolia,* serviceberry 6
6.50 *Mertensia platyphylla,* western bluebell 12
6.50 *Maianthemum stellatum,* little smilacina 10
6.67 *Claytonia linearis,* aquatic claytonia 3
6.67 *Claytonia parviflora,* small-flowered claytonia 9
6.70 *Fraxinus latifolia,* Oregon ash 10
6.73 *Lithophragma parviflora,* prairie star 11
6.75 *Ceanothus cuneatus,* common buckbrush 12
6.75 *Claytonia sibirica,* Siberian miner's lettuce 12
6.83 *Barbarea orthoceras,* American wintercress 6
6.83 *Triphysaria pusilla,* dwarf owl-clover 6
7.00 *Quercus garryana,* Oregon white oak 6
7.09 *Cornus nuttallii,* Pacific dogwood 11
7.25 *Marah oregana,* bigroot, wild cucumber 12
7.58 *Acer circinatum,* vine maple 12
7.67 *Matricaria discoidea,* pineapple weed 12
7.83 *Carex deweyana,* Dewey's sedge 6
8.00 *Hydrophyllum tenuipes,* Pacific waterleaf 6

8.00 *Ranunculus uncinatus,* disappointing buttercup 2
8.36 *Crataegus suksdorfii,* Suksdorf's hawthorn 11
8.38 *Tolmiea menziesii,* piggy-back plant 8
8.50 *Carex obnupta,* slough sedge 6
8.55 *Sanicula crassicaulis,* pacific sanicle 11
9.00 *Carex arcta,* northern clustered sedge 1
9.00 *Luzula campestris,* field woodrush 2
9.08 *Galium aparine,* bedstraw 12
9.18 *Eschscholzia californica,* California poppy 11
9.33 *Thalictrum polycarpum,* tall western meadowrue 12

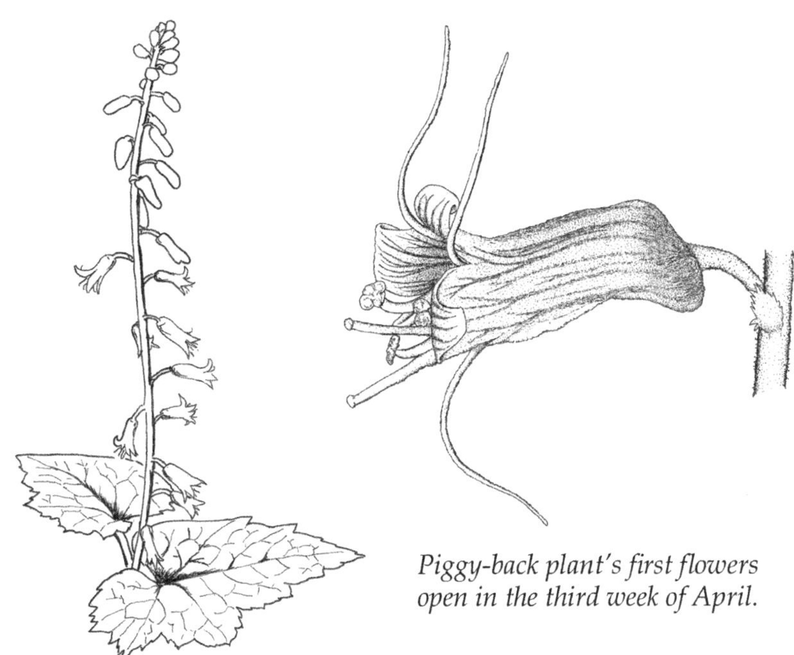

Piggy-back plant's first flowers open in the third week of April.

MAY

9.50 *Lupinus rivularis,* riverbank lupine 10
9.64 *Prunus virginiana,* chokecherry 11
10.00 *Alchemilla occidentalis,* western lady's mantle 2
10.90 *Rosa nutkana,* Nootka rose 10
11.20 *Carex stipata,* sawbeak sedge 5
11.22 *Cornus stolonifera,* redstem dogwood 9

11.38 *Poa pratensis,* Kentucky bluegrass 8
11.71 *Vicia americana,* American vetch 7
11.75 *Heracleum lanatum,* cow parship 12
11.75 *Oxalis suksdorfii,* western yellow wood sorrel 12
11.83 *Toxicodendron diversilobum,* poison oak 12
11.86 *Bromus sitchensis,* Sitka brome 7
12.09 *Symphoricarpos albus,* common snowberry 11
12.25 *Physocarpus capitatus,* ninebark 12
12.33 *Rubus parviflorus,* thimbleberry 3
12.42 *Urtica dioica,* stinging nettle 12
12.50 *Melica subulata,* onion grass 2
12.80 *Danthonia californica,* California oatgrass 5
13.00 *Dichelostemma congesta,* cluster-lily 1
13.00 *Juncus articulatus,* jointed rush 1
13.00 *Potamogeton crispus,* curly pondweed 1
13.00 *Rumix salicifolius,* willow dock 6

JUNE

13.50 *Juncus bufonius,* toad rush 6
13.50 *Myosotis laxa,* small-flower forget-me-not 2
13.75 *Juncus effusus,* common rush 4
14.00 *Glyceria elata,* tall mannagrass 1
14.00 *Satureja douglasii,* yerba buena 2
14.00 *Veronica americana,* water speedwell 1
14.17 *Elymus canadensis,* Canadian ryegrass 6
14.33 *Ranunculus aquatilis,* white water buttercup 3
14.50 *Philadelphus lewisii,* Pacific mock-orange 6
14.75 *Achillea milllefolium,* yarrow 4
15.00 *Festuca rubra,* red fescue 1
15.00 *Gnaphalium palustre,* lowland cudweed 1
16.00 *Oenanthe sarmentosa,* water-parsley 2

Our wild iris, Iris tenax, *is known as Oregon flag.*

What Is "Natural" in Natural History?

I hiked into the Three Sisters Wilderness for a dose of solitude on the last day in September. It's a little late in the year for backpacking for most folks. The days are short, the nights cold, and the weather is always chancy. On the plus side, the mosquitoes are gone and the hunter and hiker traffic is at a minimum. To optimize my chances for solitude, I drove four miles up a stony jeep track and then hiked a good seven miles to a secret spot some distance off the trail. I did choose a place at high elevation. If I really wanted to guarantee solitude, I would have tucked myself in next to a middle elevation, nondescript lake. I opted for a high-class spot with a comfy tent site and a glorious view. It proved to be the good choice; I pretty much got what I wanted.

Wilderness solitude is important to me because this is the condition I need to let my spiritual urges free. It is a situation where there is no difference between doing science and doing worship. I am such a cynical agnostic that the only place I allow these thoughts is when I feel free of any sign of human influence. In the solitude of wilderness I can ignore all beliefs about the divine or the meaning of life and simply enjoy the creation for its own sake. The creation, to me, is synonymous with the natural world. My interaction with it is emotional, visceral, spiritual, and ultimately inarticulate. So I can't write much about it.

But I do have plenty of articulate thoughts during these experiences. Sitting next to the stove making coffee in the morning, I contemplated what I mean when I refer to the natural world. Wouldn't it seem to be the same kind of "natural" as when I talk of Natural History? There is a problem for me because my definition of the natural world would seem to be the aspects of the earth that exist without human intervention. Yet, the University of Oregon Museum of Natural and Cultural History, like many other museums, focuses on the study of humans through the eyes of the discipline of anthropology. If anthropology is a subdiscipline of Natural History, then I need to modify my notion of "natural." The key to my dilemma, I think, is to recognize that humans are a natural part of the natural world.

What makes me uncomfortable about human influences, which sometimes strike me as unnatural, is that my moral and aesthetic sensibilities are a part of a personal belief system rather than logically definable phenomena. I love the beauty and diversity of nature. I am upset when these values are destroyed by motives I dislike. I was raised to believe that greed and wastefulness are wicked urges. People who misuse natural resources are, in my mind, moved by these urges. I cannot help wanting to oppose these kinds of people.

Even though I am a naturalist who considers that his profession is one of science, my environmentalism comes from a moral sense outside of science. I won't convince people to conserve nature by scientific reasoning. My environmentalist agenda is going to have to come from seeking out and cheering on people who, in their own personal way, share my morals and aesthetics. It is with these folks that I will share the location of the secret wilderness lake I went to this year.

Ice storms are as hard on plants as snow storms.

What Snow Storms Teach Us About Our Forests

Winter snow storms have had a bigger impact on Lane County as the vicissitudes of climate change increase. These storms can shut down roads and keep folks close to home. People often lose electricity after the wet, heavy snow causes branches to fall on power lines. Shut off from power and travel, they are forced to become self reliant. Eventually, the branches brought down by the storm will be gathered up to build fires to keep warm when the next storm hits. The affliction generates the cure.

After the last snow storm the caretaker of the Mount Pisgah Arboretum observed that the majority of the damage occurred to the deciduous trees—the oaks, maples, and Oregon ash. Another term for these deciduous trees is hardwoods. However, their hard wood seems to make them more vulnerable to damage than the soft wood of the Douglas-fir and true fir. The caretaker's comments made me think again about how our climate has shaped the character of our forests. It is a lesson taught to me over many years. Early in my botanical career, I hosted one of my major mentors on a trip into northern Idaho. His home territory was in the forests of the eastern U.S., rich in diversity of hardwoods. As we looked over the dense sea of greencaps from a high point, he said to me, "What a paleozoic landscape!" His exclamation was based on the observation that, although in a temperate zone, like his home state of Michigan, what dominated the hillsides in Idaho were cone-bearing trees, trees whose close ancestors dominated the earth millions of years before the hardwoods arrived on the scene. Conifers were on the hillsides before dinosaurs rose up out of the swamps. Moving from swamps to arctic ridges in paleozoic times, conifers evolved a structure for later ages. These trees of venerable lineage dominate the forests of Oregon too. Douglas-fir and hemlock, western red cedar and silver fir, white pine and spruce: these are the trees of our mountains. Why don't we have our ridges covered with maples and birches, oaks and sweet gums, sycamores and ashes? The snow has part of the answer.

Conifer trees like Douglas-fir and spruce have adapted to snow falling on their branches. They have a slender and steep profile, so that when the snow falls on them, it sloughs off as the branches tip gracefully downwards. There is a single, central trunk with a sharp point held stiffly upwards, surrounded by small, radiating branches at the top, and gradually longer, downward pointing branches arranged below. That's the physical structure that accepts snowy seasons. The oaks and ash and maples have a branch structure that angles upwards and outwards. It's great for a big load of broad leaves to catch the sun's rays in spring and summer. But it also catches a big load of snow in the off season. When the snow load comes too fast and heavy, the branches can't handle it and break. The vulnerability of these spreading, hardwood trees was demonstrated in the recent snow fall. Even more vulnerable are broadleaf evergreen trees, like madrone and tanoak. These trees are abundant only to the south of us where heavy snowfall is less frequent.

This is the physical part of why conifers like Douglas-fir dominate our forests. There's a physiological aspect that is likewise tied to our climate.

All the conifers around here are evergreen. There are evergreen hardwoods, too, but they are not common in this area. Our infrequent but regularly occurring snowfalls put them at too great a disadvantage. Having the wrong shape for snow is bad enough. If they had leaves on the branches at the time of a snowfall, the load would be unbearable. Where snow is less common, broadleaf evergreen trees are more common. That's why broadleaf evergreens such as madrone, live oak, tanoak, chinkapin, and Oregon myrtle thrive in southwest Oregon.

The physiology part that's important to conifer dominance has to do with adaptation to our Mediterranean climate. Evergreen trees are favored where winters are mild and moist while summers are hot and dry. The best time to grow is in the wet season. At low elevations in Lane County, winter is replaced by a rainy season that stitches together fall and spring. Our conifers are making food—doing photosynthesis—whenever temperatures are above freezing (or even to a few degrees below). If the temperature falls below freezing at night, it doesn't matter. There's no sunlight for photosynthesis at night anyway. Water is the main thing that limits plants' ability to grow. In this region water is scarce only in the late summer. During the typical annual drought period, all the conifers just shut down and wait for the fall rains.

Because broad leafed hardwoods lose their leaves in winter, they depend entirely on summer sunshine for growth. They really can't afford to shut down. This puts them at a distinct disadvantage on the dry mountainsides and ridgetops. Instead, they are largely confined to valley bottoms where their roots can reach a water table maintained by streams and rivers. Only here does their ability to grow faster than conifers give them the advantage.

Upslope, where the soil is mainly wetted by winter rains, the conifers are most active. Researchers working out of the Andrews Experimental Forest found that Douglas-fir needles double in size and weight during the winter. Only when the weather warms up in spring do they transport the carbohydrates down the trunks to be converted into board feet. Conifers rule the mountains around Eugene!

The call of a varied thrush consists of long, single notes at various pitches, like a squeaky wheel.

The One in Twenty Rule

There are several cases from the past where well-meaning botanists, in the pursuit of increasing knowledge about plants, have driven a species to extinction at certain sites by documenting their discoveries with collections. The case most familiar to me concerns one of the world's rarest ferns, *Botrychium pumicola*, the pumice grape fern. A student searching for new sites found two plants on Tumalo Mountain in 1954. He proudly collected them, digging them up to make complete herbarium specimens. In the late 1970s I searched the top of Tumalo Mountains with friends. We all had experienced eyes, but no plants were found. My belief is that the two plants removed in 1954 eliminated the possibility of establishment of a population of this fern. We hope that this won't happen today, that botanists finding only one or two plants would document their discovery with photographs and notes. Good photographs and careful field notes are increasingly acceptable for recording plant discoveries.

Nevertheless, from time to time a field worker is likely to encounter a small population of an unknown plant and feel it is necessary to collect a bit of it for positive identification and documentation. The Native Plant Society of Oregon's Guidelines and Ethical Codes for botanists urge that a collector use good judgement and rules of thumb when deciding whether or not to collect. What is a good rule of thumb? When this question came up at a rare plant conference many years ago I had no answer. By the late 1980s I began using a rule of thumb which I now call the "One in Twenty Rule."

Simply put, the "One in Twenty Rule" means that a botanist

If you need to collect a plant, be sure it is from a population of at least twenty.

should never collect more than one out of twenty plants. In other words, you should not collect one plant until you have found at least twenty. This runs counter to the traditional collector's mentality. As a teenage fern collector, the sight of a rare fern sent my hand out to pluck it from the rocks as a prize. Having the plant safely in my vasculum, I started looking around for more. Now, if I run across an unusual plant I suppress my traditional impulse and first think, "Can I find twenty?" Only if twenty are found will I consider collecting one plant. Forty should be present before two are taken. This applies to parts of plants too—remove no more than five percent (one twentieth) of a shrub, one frond from a clump of twenty, or five percent of a patch of moss. I use the "One in Twenty Rule" whether I am doing rare plant work or gathering common species for educational use. I now make a point to call myself a field botanist rather than a plant collector.

The "One in Twenty Rule" does not obviate the need for good judgement. Only when a botanist has the knowledge to assess if collecting is both ecologically justified and legally permitted should a specimen be taken.

One population geneticist I consulted pointed out that repeated collecting under the "One in Twenty Rule" would tend to reduce every population to nineteen individuals. This caution serves to emphasize that the "One in Twenty Rule" is a rule of thumb, not a license to ravage. Shortly after I published the "One in Twenty" idea in the newsletter of the Botanical Society of America I received a letter from James Grimes of the New York Botanical Garden asking whether I had gotten the idea from a similar article he and several other botanists had promoted in the newsletter of the Idaho Native Plant Society some years earlier. I honestly believe I did not see that publication. Then, in 1994, four botanists from Australia and New Zealand published an article in the international journal, Taxon, which made essentially the same recommendation.

My paper was republished, with minor revisions, in a number of newsletters over the next several years. Eventually Adolf Ceska placed it in an issue of BEN, an electronic newsletter, where it was noticed by Dan Branton of Canada. Dan sent me an article he had written for a local newsletter that promulgated exactly the same notion: use one in twenty as a collecting rule of thumb. He assured me that he had arrived at the notion quite spontaneously. Thus, four botanists or groups of botanists, deliberating independently, arrived at the same standard. I submit that this independent, unconscious concurrence from four separate sources speaks strongly for the sensibility of the "One in Twenty Rule."

One Look Is Worth a Thousand Pictures

My son John and I were driving to the Cherry Creek trailhead for a hike into the Sky Lakes Wilderness south of Crater Lake when we saw three squirrels running around in the road. I assumed they were playing, scampering in all directions. One raced down the middle of the road straight towards us and then veered sharply to hop off the right side of the road. The other two ran in circles, chasing one another, or so it seemed.

These two tumbled over each other in the middle of the road. I hit the brakes and we stopped to watch. John said that the backs of the squirrels were different colors. His comment made me notice the round, orange-banded ears of one of the players, and I recognized instantly that this one was a weasel. It had gripped its prey tightly from behind as they rolled over and over. I shouted, "That's a weasel!" Just then it jumped away and leaped across into the brush at the edge of the road.

We had watched it grapple with its prey and jump away just after giving the fatal bite. The plump little squirrel thrashed around in death throes. And for good reason! It would soon be dinner. The weasel just wanted us to go away.

I pulled around the victim and continued driving up the road. It was not our place to interfere with the event. We were fortuitous observers, in the right place at the right time to watch the hunt take place. We were in the front seat of a natural happening. Unlike a TV nature show, where we sit in our easy chair and watch a cheetah race down an antelope, this time it was right in

The fox squirrel, so common in our cities, is not an Oregon native.

front of us and we could smell the dust of the struggle.

When I got home I checked my books to verify what we had seen. It had been a longtail weasel. This predator is much smaller than our urban squirrels. It is found throughout the state, hunting by day more than most small predators. The Peterson Field Guide to the Mammals confirmed, too, that it "kills by piercing (the) skull with canines." The grim reality of nature? Reality, yes; grim, only depending on one's sensitivities.

As John and I hiked up the Cherry Creek trail looking for mushrooms, I reflected on the lessons to be learned from what we had witnessed. The woods were too dry for most mushrooms, so I had time to think. The truth of impermanence first fell in front of me: each individual life is transient. It's one of those self-evident truths not mentioned in the Declaration of Independence and all too easily overlooked in political times of self-promotion. Then there's the paradox of benefits: what kills one feeds another. It leads to questions about the morality of intervention—if I'd had a chance to save a squirrel, would that have been a goodwill effort for that environment?

I had many more thoughts as we paced for the three or four miles of mushroom deficient trail. I appreciated the simple grace of our experience. We had been there to see it. I have described it in a few words. Pictures would help a lot. The longtail weasel is a most graceful creature; the golden mantled squirrel is incredibly cute. You know, "a picture is worth a thousand words." There is no way to express, to communicate to my friends, all the significance of witnessing the weasel catch its squirrel. You have to see it.

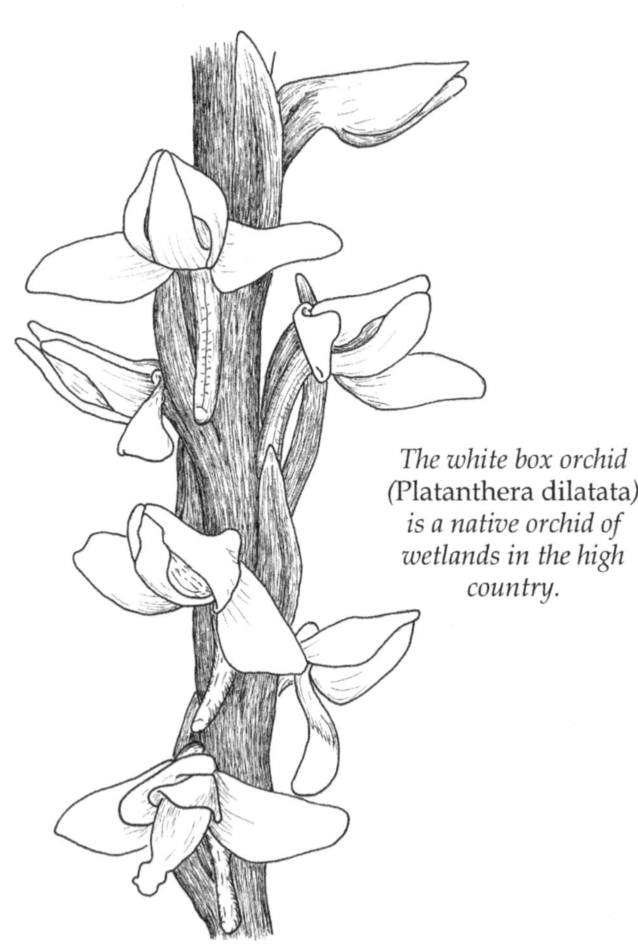

The white box orchid (Platanthera dilatata) *is a native orchid of wetlands in the high country.*

Comments on the "Sounds of Silence"

After the 9/11 attacks on the World Trade Center and other targets in 2001, all aircraft in the country were grounded for a day. I was in the heart of the Three Sisters Wilderness at the time, camping with my daughter. It's interesting to me that I really didn't notice the absence of jet noise. Only in hindsight did it occur to me that part of my enjoyment of the wilderness was the silence. I learned of the event only days later. Curiously, I am annoyed by the sound of jets but did not notice their absence. This has made me think about my personal appreciation of nature. It is almost completely visual. I tend to ignore or underappreciate my other senses. Sounds are not that important to somebody who focuses on mosses, flowers, and butterflies. My birding friends, on the other hand (on the other ear?), are always attuned to the sound of bird calls. A geologist has a good sense of specific gravity when hefting a stone; an archaeologist feels the subtleties of artifacts. As a botanist, I use my sense of touch only when feeling the stems of a pair of similar species of desert parsley: one is rough and the other smooth.

My most underappreciated sense is smell. People who have been on nature walks with me have heard me describe my son as a "noser." Ever since he was a small child, he'd put things to his nose to smell them. I never did that automatically. When I want to observe something closely, I put it under my hand lens. Only in the past ten years or so have I been an active noser, since I became interested in mushrooms. Only by smell can I positively identify such delectables as a matsutake or The Prince. I envy the skill of Rob Weiss, a botanist who has worked so closely with trees that he can detect the difference among various species of true firs by their smell. I've tried to match his accomplishment and have not yet succeeded.

What about taste? Some people are constant tasters, but this is not always a good trait. Jay Marston, late Lane Community College instructor, told of a taster in one of his classes. Standing in a wetland, Jay noticed her nibbling on a stem of water hemlock, one of our most poisonous plants. The rest of the trip was spent getting her to an emergency room to have her stomach pumped. I do not encourage indiscriminate tasting, but I have to admit there is one species of liverwort that I identify positively in the field with a taste test. The peppery Porella is hot on the tip of the tongue while its look-alikes are simply bland or lightly aromatic.

The ability to use all of my senses is a gift I didn't fully appreciate until the day the jets were silent.

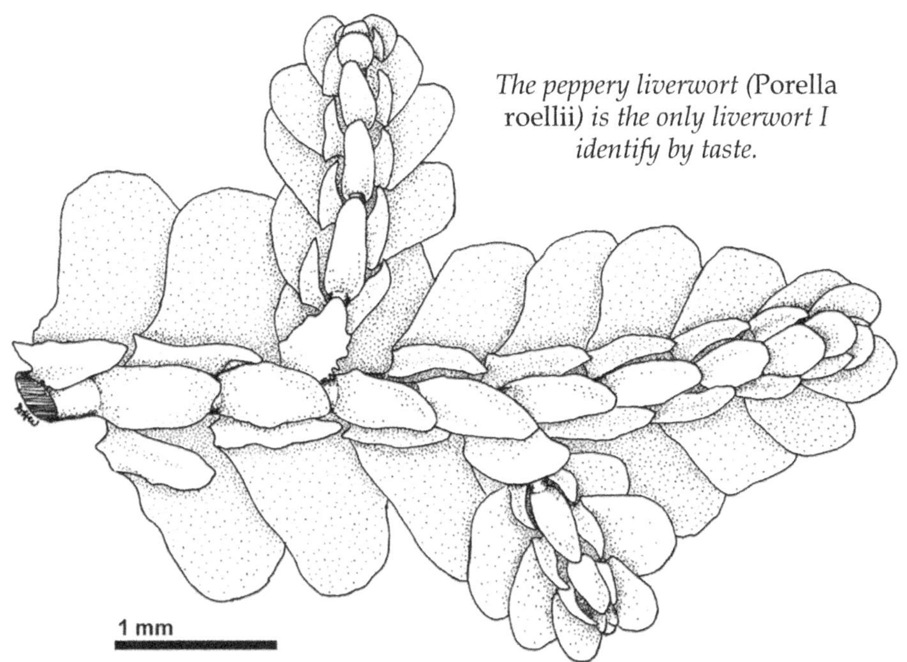

*The peppery liverwort (*Porella roellii*) is the only liverwort I identify by taste.*

Times Change

England has finally banned fox hunting with hounds. I always thought it was a bit funny to call it hunting—releasing a pack of dogs to find, track, and then kill a fox, all the while chasing after the dogs on horses. It comes as no surprise that this cruel vestige of aristocracy was outlawed after years of opposition by the plain folk of the land. It reminded me of changes that have occurred in my own life, as I too moved beyond a traditional British way of doing things.

In my youth in India I was an avid butterfly collector. It was a holdover hobby from the British era. The school I went to was run by American missionaries, but had previously been a British boarding school. Collecting butterflies was a very proper hobby for a young boy there. I felt I was following in the footsteps of Charles Darwin. Indeed, I was. After returning to the U.S. for college I made myself a new net and took up butterfly collecting again. However, this activity never regained the intensity of my teenage years, and gradually I stopped catching butterflies for fun. The end of collecting came when Robert Michael Pyle published Watching Washington Butterflies. After that I took up binoculars for butterfly studies, just as birders do for birds.

My older brother, who had once hunted mammals and collected birds as a hobby, similarly turned to a camera before he left India in the mid-1950s. Nobody today would imagine killing and collecting songbirds for fun. A century ago, however, collecting bird nests and bird eggs was all the craze. Times change.

The lesson from this is that change is an important part of our culture's maturation in its outlook towards nature. The ranchers and loggers who complain about losing the old ways are going to be lost in the dust of the modern rancher and timber managers. Like a grizzled old cowboy, I have moments when I get nostalgic over the old days. My nostalgia was particularly strong the day I ran across a poem I wrote at the age of seventeen, as a senior in high school. It was written for an English composition class, and I have to thank my mother for saving it.

WHERE THE BUTTERFLIES LAND

See that rock there? That's where I'll stand.
Just below that's where butterflies land.
You place yourself where they all come to drink.
You have to watch close because if you blink
You'll miss the fast ones, they fly straight by.
From here I can catch the ones flying high,
I'll shout if I see one coming in low.
I have noticed before these often are slow.
So just take your time and don't swing too fast;
Swing 'round from behind just as they have passed.
This way you can catch them and not break their wings.
You'll soon have the timing for all of your swings.
There's one now! Up on that bush.
Quick! Step in my hands! I'll give you a push
To get up on this rock; from there you can catch it.
Hold on with one hand, lean out just a bit.
There, now you can reach. Swing fast! Now twist!
That's it! You have it! That's using your wrist!
Don't let it flutter. It's not hard to kill.
Just give it a pinch and it will lie still.
This is a good one, which is quite hard to get.
The ones which I caught were torn in my net.
These ones are rare. I have caught very few;
Just down from here I got one or two.
We are lucky today to get one so soon.
We'll catch around here and then about noon

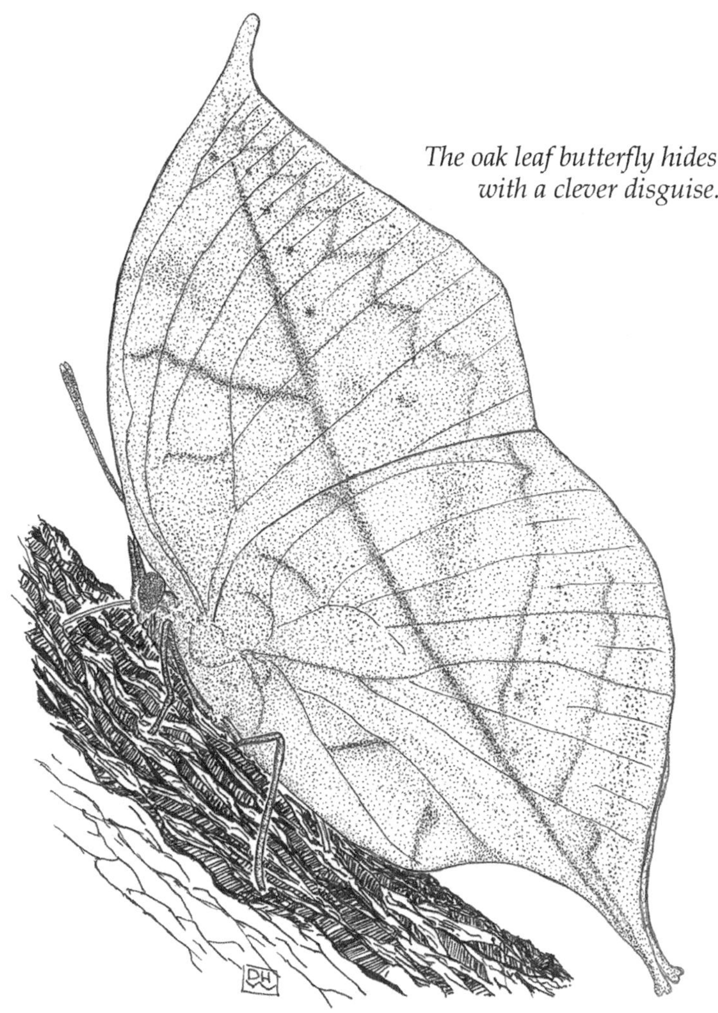

The oak leaf butterfly hides with a clever disguise.

We'll go down and eat by the waterfall's pool.
I know a place that's shady and cool
From where we can see all that passes by.
That time of day I find that they fly
A little more slowly and often will dip
Down to rest on the sand for a second to sip
A few drops of water. Hey! How about that!
This little brown one tried to sit on my hat.
Well, his wing is torn so I'll let him go.
I don't like to kill ones which I know
I won't put away. What's that over there?

He's up in a place where you can tear
Your net on the thorns. There he goes—to that limb.
That is much better—Ha! I nabbed him.
Come here, take a look! I'm glad you're with me.
It is much more fun to let someone see
What you catch, right away, while you're still thrilled.
The deep satisfaction with which you are filled
When you snare a prize is never as great as
When you're not alone. I find the trip has
Much more success when I have a friend who collects with me.

—April, 1963

If you see a small blue butterfly in the Cascade Range, it is probably Plebejus acmon, *known simply as a "blue".*

Frugalism

On the first day of class for Field Botany at the University of Oregon summer school I passed out press boards to the students. I explained proudly that the press boards are recycled. I cut them from leftover plywood scraps. I had no need to buy new sheets of plywood to make the twenty-four sets of boards required for this class.

I explained, "This is a demonstration of Wagner's Second Law of Frugalism. Never buy new when you can make do."

One student asked, "Shouldn't this be the First Law of Frugalism?"

"No," I replied, "the First Law of Frugalism is 'Never throw anything away.'"

There was a good laugh after this exchange. I did hope that, at least for some in the class, there was a valuable lesson to be learned. Being frugal is a moral aspect of learning about nature. Moral aspects are a guarded, even subversive side of teaching science.

My job in teaching Field Botany is to train students how to identify the plants they come across. Students pay good money to learn this valuable and technical skill. Scientists need to know how to put a name on the organisms they investigate. What a thing is—its name—tells you its relationships: ecological, genetical, evolutionary, and even economical. In the realm of natural resource economy, frugalism is a moral force.

So, how does a specialist in natural history express frugalism? A frugalist is a person who believes that waste is a moral disor-

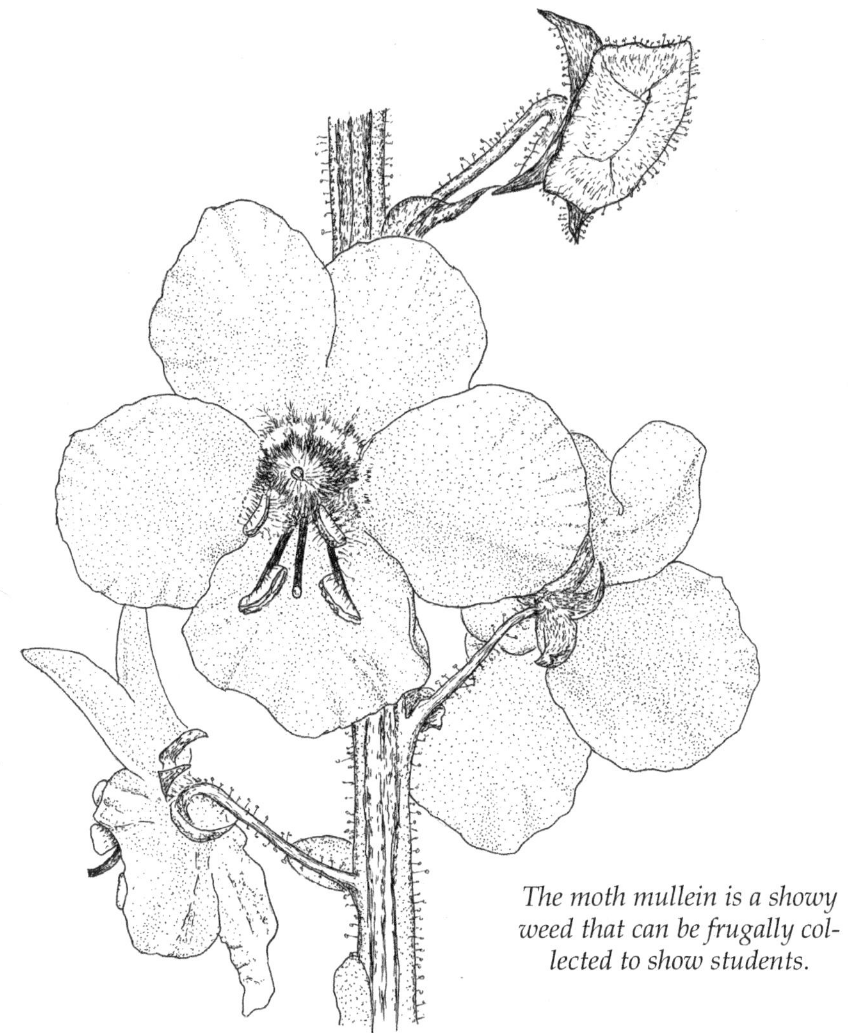

The moth mullein is a showy weed that can be frugally collected to show students.

der. If Frugalism were a religion, waste would be the grossest sin. I do not think Frugalism will ever qualify as a religion. But I do believe it qualifies as a virtue in most religious world views.

So I practice a frugal approach to my teaching of field botany. I avoid excessive copying from textbooks and keep handouts to a minimum. I tell the students to pay attention to what I say and what I draw on the board, because it might not be covered in handouts. Study the specimens I bring to lab. Listen, look, and learn.

I do not send students out to gather everything they see to

bring into class for study. I know what each lesson requires and I bring exactly what is appropriate. I never pull up a whole plant for a demonstration when a single flower or leaf will do. The Third Law of Frugalism could be, "Don't take what you don't need."

To preserve the natural world we need to be conservative about how we exploit our natural resources. To be frugal with our natural resources is the highest moral stand. It astounds me that in the political realm, people who strive to conserve our natural resources for public benefit are called "liberals" while those who would exploit our natural resources for private gain are called the "conservatives." Where is the moral compass in that nomenclature?

Showy phlox (Phlox speciosa) *is rare enough in Oregon that it should not be collected casually.*

Pressing and Mounting Leaves

Pressed and mounted leaves are not merely useful as scientific specimens, but can also make attractive fall decorations. The critical part of the process is to dry the leaves quickly while they are being pressed. I use a plant press made from boards, ropes, and newspapers. Start by cutting two 9″ X 12″ sheets of 3/8″ plywood for the end boards. The leaves will be pressed between newspapers bound inside these press boards.

Set one press board on a table and place several folded sheets of newspaper on it. Arrange leaves in a newspaper folder so the leaves do not overlap. Build up a stack of alternating layers of leaves in folders. Five to ten folders of leaves are a good number to handle at one time. Then put the second press board on top. Finally bundle the whole collection tightly with rope, or press it under a board with a weight.

How well the leaves are pressed is determined by how tightly the press bundle is tied. Here's a trick that helps. Place a one-inch thick sheet of polyurethane foam on top of the press. If the foam is compressed while tying, it keeps excellent pressure on the whole stack. I put a knee on the press, between the ropes, while tying up the press.

Pressing is only half of the process; the other half is drying. This is done by changing the blotters. The newspaper blotters draw moisture out of the leaves. After only a few hours, the newspapers have drawn about as much moisture out of the leaves as they can absorb quickly. It is time to replace the blotter in the press with dry blotters.

Open the press, set aside the foam (if you are using some),

and put the top press board on the right. Put a dry newspaper blotter on this board. Take the moist newspaper off the stack in the press and set it to the left side. Transfer the leaves from the press stack to the dry newspaper. Put a dry blotter on the transferred leaves. Then remove the next moist blotter from the press stack and set that aside. Repeat the leaf transfer process until all the leaves in the press have been transferred to the new stack of leaves and dry newspapers on the right. Replace the foam and tighten the press.

Most leaves will dry in a few days if the newspapers are changed in the press twice daily, To test for dryness, hold a leaf against your lips. If it feels like a piece of paper, it is dry. If it feels cool, there is still moisture in the leaf that is drawing heat from your lips, and a few more changes of dry newspaper in the press are needed before mounting.

When drying is completed, arrange the leaves as artistically as you choose on a sheet of heavy mounting paper or cardstock.

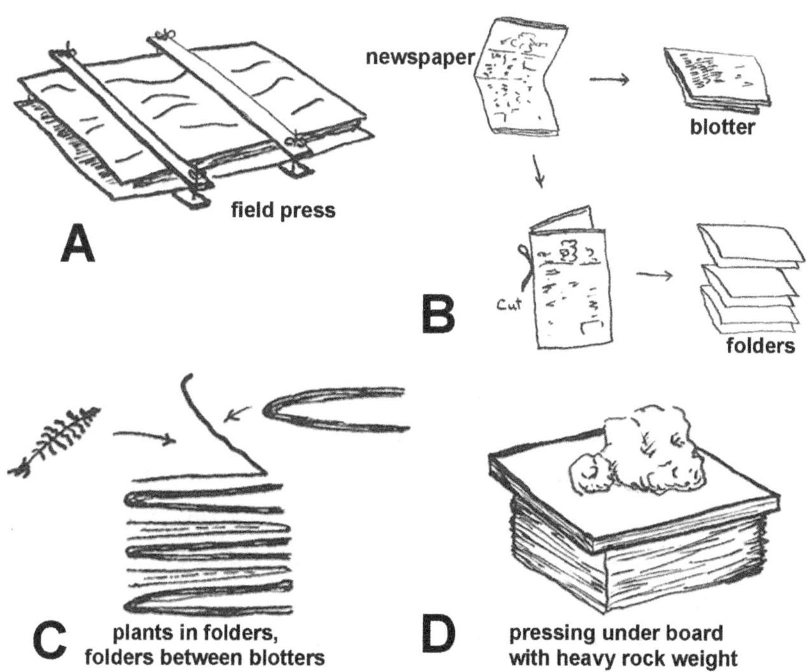

Pressing plants is an easy and fun project.

When you are satisfied with the arrangement, apply glue. A white glue like Elmer's works very well. First use a two-inch paint brush to spread a thin layer of glue on a sheet of glass, formica, metal or other smooth, hard surface. Thin the glue with a few drops of water to help spread it out. Experience will instruct how much water to use. Start with a thin layer of thinned glue.

Pick up a leaf by the base with a pair of sharp tweezers (forceps) and set the leaf carefully on the thin layer of glue. Poke the leaf down onto the glue plate with a fingertip to be sure the underside of the leaf gets an even coating of glue.

Use the forceps again to pick up the leaf by the base next to the leaf stalk. Lift carefully so the glue stays on the underside of the leaf. Set the leaf down on the sheet of mounting paper. If there is so much glue that it squeezes out from the side of the leaf, blot the edges with a paper towel or bath tissue.

I like to set the glue under pressure. To do this, lay the sheet with the freshly glued leaf on a section of newspaper. Then carefully lay a piece of plastic wrap over the leaf. This keeps the glue from sticking to anything except the mounting sheet. Lay a newspaper on top of this, then a press board, then a weight—I like to use a two-gallon bucket filled with gravel.

The next mounted leaf is added to this stack by lifting off the weight and board, then adding the sheet with leaf placed on top of the newspaper. Add another piece of plastic wrap, another newspaper, and then replace the board and weight. Mounting continues in this fashion and ensures that the glue will have its moisture drawn through the mounting sheet into the newspaper below. The plastic wrap keeps the leaf mount from sticking to the newspaper above it in the stack.

This stack needs to be left alone for a couple of hours; overnight is ideal. By then the plastic wrap will have set up in the white glue. Peel off the plastic and set the sheets in the open to finish drying. If the paper curls up at this stage, either the mounting sheet was too flimsy or you used too much glue. After final drying, the mounted leaves are suitable for display or making rubbings.

*Bearberry (*Arctostaphylos uva-ursi*) is a native evergreen ground cover that provides bright red berries in addition to winter greens.*

Winter Greens

Midwinter usually brings an abundance of rainy weather to the Willamette Valley. Dark clouds and the splatter of raindrops on the roof give some people the winter blues. But not me, because I'm paying attention to the plant world. Thanks to the rain and the lengthening days of January, our vegetable friends are feeling positively perky. Buds are swelling and leaves are pushing out of the ground. So I get the winter greens, not the winter blues.

Some of our plants are already beginning their season of seeding. Seeds are the plant's next generation, encapsulated in suspended animation within a seed coat. The seeding process begins with fertilization. The earliest plants just sprinkle their sperm cells, protected by a weatherproof coating, on the wind.

We call these cells pollen. Among the first plants to pollinate are the incense cedars. In January their male (pollen) cones are already falling to the ground by the thousands. Their pollen dispersed, the male cones' job is done. They quickly shrivel and are torn from branch tips by the winter winds. In a few weeks, the female seed cones that failed to be fertilized by pollen will themselves fall in a dramatic "baby cone" drop. The pregnant seed cones take all summer to mature and shed seeds only in the fall.

Another plant that sheds its pollen early is the cultivated filbert, which is marketed as hazelnut. It's important to distinguish this horticultural crop from the wild, native filbert. The differences are slight and, given the chance, they will interbreed. What keeps them apart in most circumstances is timing. Cultivated filberts elongate male catkins in January. The wild filbert doesn't do its fertilizing until a month or more later, so natural cross breeding is rare.

A catkin is a long, dangly male cone. Just like the incense cedar, the male catkins of filberts eject millions of pollen grains into the air. The pollen grains carry their male genes to the shy stigmas of the female flowers. Because filbert flowers do not need to attract insects, they are not showy. They have long, feathery stigmas that sweep pollen out of the air. The stigmas are bright red, so a careful observer can usually find them on a tree along with the flagrant display of male catkins.

Some of us first learn that pollination is underway because filbert pollen causes allergic reactions. Not nearly as many people are sensitive to filbert pollen as to grass pollen. The truly sensitive will tell you that the hay fever season in the Willamette Valley begins in January.

Wind pollinated plants are prominent in our area. Like filberts, grasses are pollinated by wind. All the conifers are wind pollinated. Many of our deciduous trees are wind pollinated too - oaks, ash, alders, and cottonwoods. All of these have catkins or clusters of naked male flowers that shed huge quantities of pollen into the air. All perform pollination before the leaves appear on the branches, so that the leaves don't interfere with the movement of pollen on air currents. The trees that use insects for pollination, like bigleaf maple and the Pacific dogwood, produce leaves and flowers at about the same time, much later than the wind pollinated ones. Willows are a special case, unusual in many ways. They have catkins but are insect pollinated. Depending on the species, their catkins may appear before, at the same time, or much later than their leaves.

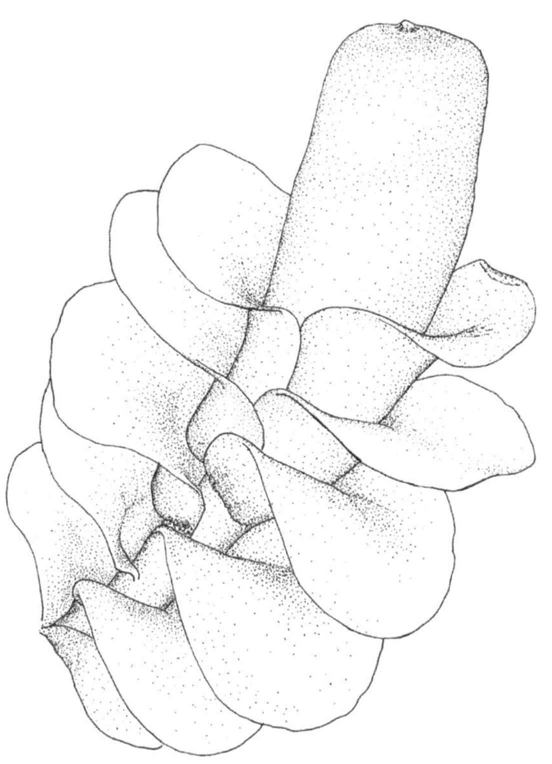

This long-leaf flapwort is ready for fertilization.

Winter greens sweep over me when I contemplate my favorite plants, the mosses and liverworts. All of them are in a fertilizing frenzy in January. They do not encapsulate their sperm in pollen. These "lower" plants have swimming sperm. Fertilization requires the sperm to swim through an aqueous medium, usually rainwater, to get to the egg flasks. Winter is the best time of the year for this activity. The products of moss fertilization won't be visible until next winter. The young embryos of moss sporelings remain tiny and dormant all summer. The spore capsules we see this season are a result of fertilizations that took place last spring.

So, don't suffer from the winter blues. Put on your raincoat and go out to celebrate the winter greens.

Natural History from Urban to Wild

Appreciation of nature often begins in one's own backyard. Hearing birds sing before getting out of bed, and knowing which birds are singing, is the typical start of a nature lover's day. Caring for the preservation of nature around our home is a personal matter. It is a personal choice to put out bird feeders and keep the cat indoors. It is a personal choice to plant native species in our gardens. Caring for the preservation in the world at large is where organizations and agencies come in. The basic premise of environmental organizations is that each of us who loves nature has a moral obligation to protect and preserve natural areas for future generations to enjoy as we have.

I think most environmentalists think of "the wild" when asked to think of the conservation of nature. I certainly have great affection for wilderness areas, places where I can connect with the processes of nature where signs of human impact are minimal. People like me place great importance on preserving as large a swath of wilderness as our culture will allow. We know that to maximize the preservation of wilderness, we need to encourage the appreciation of nature in as wide a segment of society as possible. That so many people in our society do not appreciate nature, that so many look upon the natural world solely as a source of resources to be exploited, is a serious cultural challenge.

Our best hope is to educate as many people as possible, in all kinds of places. Natural areas in neighborhood parks are the true front line. Our city has an active program of habitat rehabilitation in urban parks. The Delta Ponds, just north of Valley River Center along the riverbank bike path, were originally nothing more than flooded gravel pits left after highway construction. With care, they have become an excellent example of a popular urban preserve. It is hard to imagine somebody pedaling down the path and not stopping to take in the beauty of these ponds.

Particularly important are programs that introduce children to nature, such as the classes held by Nearby Nature in Alton Baker Park. We need to get "them" while they're young! Most schools have an outdoor education component in their curriculum. The urban natural areas are a vital resource for this element of education. I think it really helps that children can be given exposure to nature study and nature appreciation in places where they can return to walk and enjoy with their families

Once people learn to love nature at home and in urban preserves, they will be ready to visit regional parks like Buford Park, and then to go on to National Forests and wilderness areas. And maybe, hopefully, they will then take part in promoting the conservation of resources on all public lands.

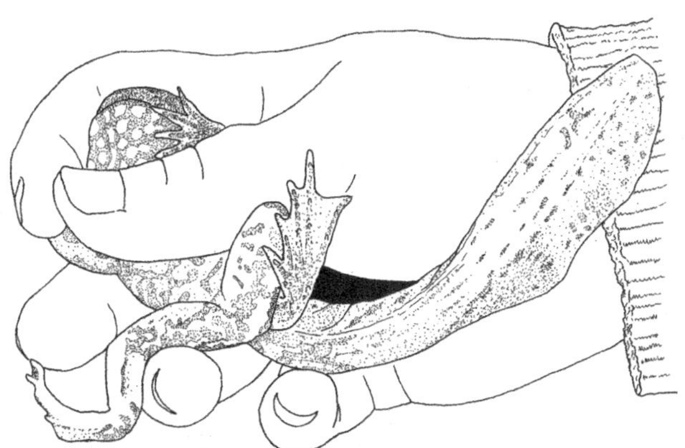

Every child deserves the chance to inspect a tadpole that is almost a frog.

Minority Viewpoints, Unpopular Theories, and Good Science

When and how were food plants introduced around the world? Because the cultivation of crops predates the beginning of written history by several thousand years, it is not easy to know where a domesticated plant first originated. Figuring out patterns of dispersal is even tougher. Archaeological evidence provides considerable insight, but the ancient record is spotty and open to different interpretations. Because of the value of agriculture, food plants spread quickly. Often it is difficult to distinguish a place of origin from a way station in species dispersal.

One of the major events in human history was the contact between the Old World and the New World. The most widely held view is that this contact was primarily initiated by the voyages of Christopher Columbus. Leif Ericson briefly placed a Norse colony on this continent but no cross-oceanic cultural exchange appears to have occurred.

It is common to refer to events as pre-Columbian or post-Columbian, before or after 1492 CE. Most scholars agree that this was a turning point for plant exchange, after which corn and potatoes were introduced in Europe, for example, and many other crops were brought to the Americas. But there are some who support alternate dispersal models, known as diffusionist theories.

As a youth I read *Kon-Tiki* several times, one of the most wonderful true life adventure stories of my generation. Thor

Heyerdahl intended to demonstrate that trans-oceanic travel by ancient methods was possible long before Columbus. This he did successfully and I have always been intrigued by the possibility. Later genetic evidence has shown that the Americas probably did not have significant contact with the Polynesians or exchange crop plants. Nonetheless, some scientists still hold to diffusionist theories.

It is interesting to note that the diffusionist model of crop dispersal is an unpopular but scientific theory, in contrast to popular theories which are not scientific. I'm thinking specifically of the intelligent design and creationist ideas. They are popular beliefs but not scientific theories.

One way to understand this is to consider the effort by some state legislatures to require that a sticker be placed in science books stating, "Evolution is a theory, not a fact." Suppose a different legislature, wanting to be balanced about science, suggested requiring that every Bible in public schools and public libraries have a sticker stating, "The existence of God is a theory, not a fact." This is, of course, an absurd notion; no legislature would make any such proposal. The existence of God is a belief and there's nothing wrong with that. It is not, however, a theory subject to scientific testing.

Evolution is a theory, and that is exactly as it should be because it is subject to scientific inquiry. Intelligent design is a belief, not a theory subject to scientific questioning. This is not to say a scientist as both a thoughtful and religious person might not believe in God as an intelligent designer; indeed, this appears to be the case as often as not.

It is important to remember that science is a process, a way to learn, and not a set of truths or confirmed knowledge. Whether or not someone "believes" in pre-Columbian dispersal is not the point. If someone is able to present verifiable evidence even for the most unpopular of theories, the process of science requires that it be evaluated with an open mind.

The Latest Scientific Discovery

Every now and then we read that a great scientific discovery has been made, opening a fresh way of looking at a long-standing mystery. We typically expect these news releases to be about advances in quantum physics, molecular biology, or low-temperature electronics. How delighted I was to read that the latest breakthrough discovery is about the natural history of mosses!

The issue has been a basic one: How are mosses able to sexually reproduce efficiently enough for evolution to occur? The problem is that mosses have the most primitive mode of reproduction among all land organisms. A sperm must swim between male and female plants, through a liquid environment external to the plants. Seed plants have solved the problem by putting their sperm cells into pollen grains and sending them through the air.

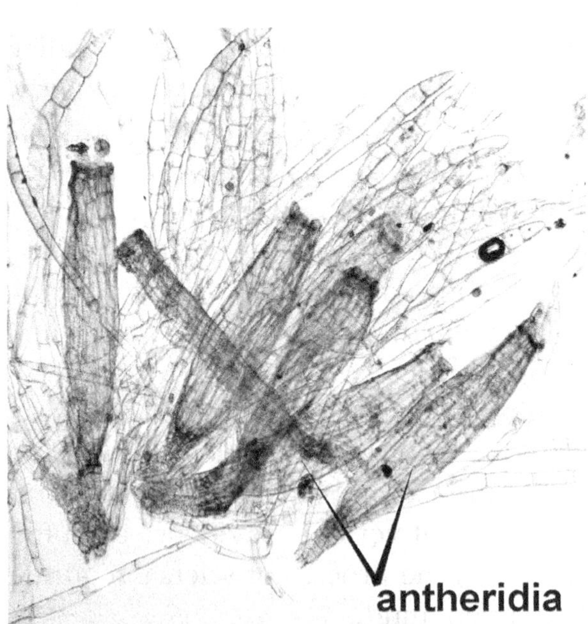

Moss antheridia are empty after releasing sperm.

Flowering plants have taken this one step further by employing insects, birds, and bats to carry pollen from one flower to another. Lacking pollen, mosses must do their best with sending their spermatozoids out into an external, watery world. A group of Swedish botanists led by Nils Cronberg recently performed an elegant experiment which demonstrates that mosses, too, can use insects to carry sperm from a male plant to a female plant.

Their experiment used a moss widespread in temperate regions of the world, the silvery bryum. It grows like a weed everywhere, even in cracks in the sidewalks in Eugene. Bulging cushions of this moss were pressure blasted off Eugene's Washington-Jefferson freeway bridges not long ago. It is a highly successful moss, yet it grows in colonies that are either all male or all female. The big question has been, "How far can sperm swim to fertilize the female plants?" Experiments attempting to measure this distance in the past have not yielded satisfying results. Moss sperm are coiled and have two long tails that slowly propel them spirally through the water. With a meager store of energy, they don't get far.

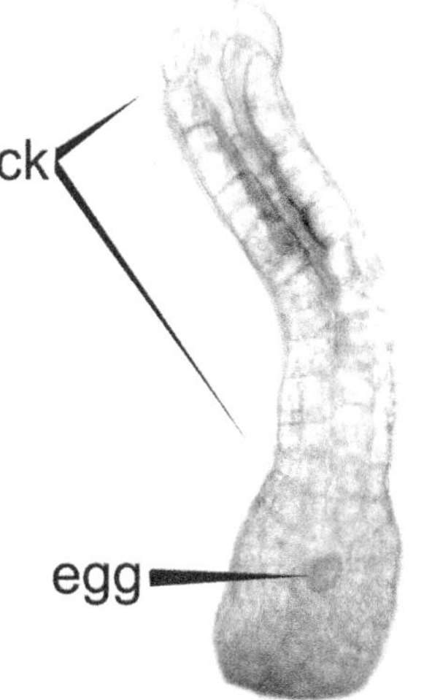

Archegonium *with egg ready to fertilize.*

What Cronberg and associates did was recognize that mosses live in an ecosystem with a panoply of other organisms around them. Observations going back more than a century noted that small insects had moss sperm stuck to them. Prominent among the coinhabitants of the moss world are springtails, primitive, tiny, wingless insects. Cronberg's group tested the ability of springtails to carry sperm between moss colonies. They poured plaster of Paris into culture dishes, poked holes in the plaster, and established small colonies of the silvery bryum there. The holes held sufficient moisture to keep the colonies healthy, but the dry surface of the plaster stopped any sperm that attempted to swim away. Colonies of male and female mosses were placed two and four centimeters apart. The scientists waited, but none of the female mosses were fertilized. None developed spore capsules.

However, when springtails were introduced into the dishes, they roamed about freely, feeding on dead organic material in various moss colonies. In the process they carried moss sperm, and within twenty hours all female colonies were well fertilized, producing abundant spore capsules at both the two and four centimeter distances. Eureka!

What makes this such a dramatic experiment is its implication in the general natural history of mosses. Springtails are very primitive insects. They have been around as long as mosses—over 300 million years. And springtails are very abundant, acting as breakdown organisms in the process of decomposition of dead plant material in almost every habitat.

This study published in Science, the most prestigious journal in the country, demonstrates that marvelous natural history discoveries are yet to be made. Moss experts are at the cutting edge of hard science!

Recognize the song sparrow by its melodius call, apparently singing, "I am a SPARROW!"

Change Blindness

Recently I had a traumatic and life-changing experience. I was building a shelter along our fence to store firewood for the winter. While using a table saw to rip a long board into narrow strips, the board fell off the stand and threw my hand back into the saw blade. The end of my right thumb disappeared faster than I could think.

The wound was nicely sewn up and now is pretty well healed. It's still sensitive but that will diminish over time. In recent days I've been thinking a lot about how much I wish that hadn't happened. According to my doctor, that's part of the grieving process over my loss. There are two obvious lessons from this event. The first one is for carpenters: Always use a push stick when using a table saw. The second one is more general: Things change and changes are permanent. No matter how much we might wish things to stay the same, most change is inexorable.

The deepest denial is probably the refusal to accept mortality. The logical part of our brain might know that youth passes into old age and old age leads to the end of life. These are inevitable changes that most of us just don't think about on a daily basis. I am one of those who believes, like the great evolutionary geneticist, Theodosius Dobzhansky, that the ability to ignore mortality is a part of our fundamental neural hard wiring that has evolved by natural selection. Whether or not this is true, the fact remains that humans have an enormous capacity to be blind to change.

Another example is the refusal of many to accept the existence of global warming. Global warming is not a single event like an earthquake, which, once it has happened, leaves clear evidence of its consequences. Global warming is an ongoing process of change. This makes its existence easier to deny.

Another example of a deep refusal to accept change is the position taken by strict creationists. These people believe the world is pretty much the way it always has been. They overlook slow, natural processes of change. Instead they prefer to believe that only sudden acts of magic bring about major changes, such as the creation of the earth in one day. It is usual to credit religious traditions as the source of creationist thinking but I think "change blindness" is at the root of it.

People who love natural history and their natural environment are not immune to this blindness. Our forests will never be the same as they were a hundred years ago. Even in a pristine area that has never been logged, the processes that shaped the ecosystem have changed. We have introduced new plants, new animals, and a new climate. Trying to maintain natural areas as if they will always be the way Europeans found them in the 1800s is futile. This is not to say we shouldn't do our best to preserve natural areas, just that it is unreasonable to expect them always to be the way we have enjoyed them. Blindness won't help. Even for ecosystems, change is inevitable.

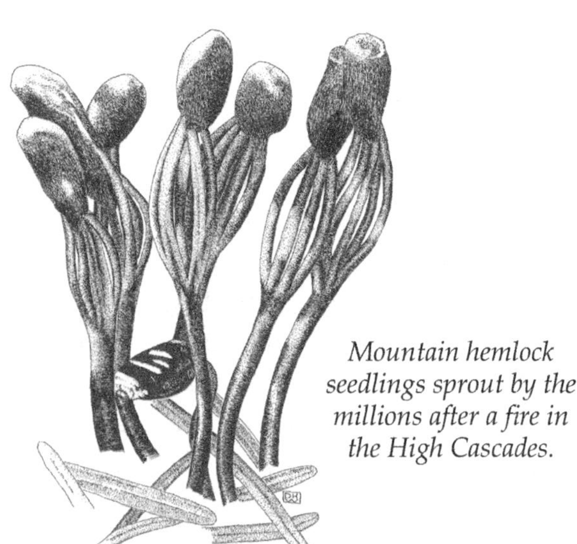

Mountain hemlock seedlings sprout by the millions after a fire in the High Cascades.

Getting to Feel at Home

On my sixty-second birthday I realized that I had lived in Eugene for exactly half my life. I arrived here during the week of my birthday in 1976. The last time I felt moved by such a milestone was in my thirties, when I passed the date that marked having spent more than half my life in the United States. The first eighteen years of my life I had been in India, where my father was a missionary.

That I'm still in Eugene is a commitment to place. At the age of forty-seven I was the director and curator of the University of Oregon Herbarium. I taught botany in the Department of Biology. But then the tax cut massacre of Measure 5 led the university to close its herbarium and terminate my position. I needed a new job. Nothing materialized for me in the Pacific Northwest, so thoughts of moving to Kansas or Tennessee for teaching positions came under consideration. Not serious consideration, however, because I felt bonded to the Cascadia bioregion. In one of his essays the poet Gary Snyder wrote, "If you want to care for the environment, put down roots." As a botanist this call had particular resonance for me. Since then I have extended my roots deeper, fortunate to be able to make a living as a freelance botanist in the region I love.

Caring for the environment means more than just becoming attached to it. If you are attached to a place, you should live in a way that shows it. Write letters to the forest supervisor protesting unwise logging. Reuse and recycle, rather than buy new. And do what you can to help more people establish a bond to the land. Everyone who has lived half their life in a place should not only love it, but help care for it.

The small, whitish seeds had mysteriously appeared on a Eugene driveway.

Mystery Seeds

Early one year Marge Zane brought me some strange objects to identify. I was pretty sure they were seeds but I didn't recognize them. I had a vague sense I'd seen them before. Marge had found them in a friend's driveway southwest of Eugene on Lorane Highway, on the west side of Spencer Butte.

First I showed them to other board members of the Eugene Natural History Society, then to the society members at large. Nobody recognized them. I took a bag of the seeds to the Wildflower Festival at the Mount Pisgah Arboretum in May and put them out on the experts' table with a sign that said, "Mystery Seeds: can you recognize them?" But nobody recognized them. One person took some home and picked them apart. He found them filled up with a larva so he guessed these objects were insect galls. He was not the only one who thought this. I sent a few seeds to experts in the Department of Botany and Plant Pathology at Oregon State University. Nobody there recognized the seeds but one botanist thought they must be insect galls. Another expert said it would be, "forever a mystery."

Well, neither Marge nor I were willing to accept "forever a mystery." Chuck Kimmel split some open and found what looked like little plant embryos. I found the same, so the seeds with larvae were undoubtedly being preyed upon by seed predators. If they were seeds, then they should grow if planted! I slapped my forehead when I thought of this. It turns out that several other ENHS board members already had this idea and had planted some of Marge's seeds. Mine were planted on May 10 and germinated by the first of June. The cotyledons were a pretty, glossy green. There were two cotyledons, so we knew it couldn't be some kind of monocot, like grasses and lilies.

While the cotyledons grew, we tried to guess what they might be. Several thought they might be mistletoe seeds, but mistletoe seeds are sticky, so they can attach to branches when carried there by birds. There was a lot of periwinkle (*Vinca*) at Marge's place and this was a hot candidate for me, at least for a while. Periwinkle has shiny leaves, just like the cotyledons of our seedlings. On a visit to Marge's house she showed us some seedlings growing right next to a big patch of periwinkle. However, the pictures of periwinkle seeds I found on the Internet didn't look right. Periwinkle seeds are intricately fissured. Ours looked like shriveled brains inside a papery coating.

At last the strange seeds germinated. But what plant was this?

Although the seeds germinated quickly enough, it took a long time for the seedlings to develop true leaves that could be identified with confidence. The critical evidence that my periwinkle theory was doomed came when leaves sprouted one at a time on the stem, not in pairs like periwinkle. In the end, it turned out that these strange, silver and pink, papery seeds are from the dried berries of English ivy. Once I knew this, it wasn't hard to find pictures of ivy seeds on the web. Arrgh! We had wanted them to be something interesting! The people who had laboriously nurtured these seeds yanked the plants out. One told me, "They grew, and they grew, and the glossy green brought pride and chatter: 'Mine have sprouted!'" Then the many inquiring souls providing sustenance and nurture suddenly cried out and swiftly exhumed the sprouting interlopers from their tiny beds, never giving them the chance to spread and spread.

More mature leaves revealed the awful truth.

I really had seen these seeds before, in my driveway here in north Eugene. Look for them, gather them, and throw them in the fireplace! This invasive ivy is a menace to native vegetation, a green horde that takes over wild places in our public parks. The Eugene Natural History Society started the tradition of pulling ivy in Alton Baker Park. Maybe we should get back into such activity. Damn the mystery seeds!

Parnassius clodius *is a white butterfly of the snow Apollo genus.*

Marching Forests and Butterflies

The impact of global warming on local ecosystems manifests itself in many ways. A recent note in *Natural History* magazine describes an effect on butterflies in the Rocky Mountains of Alberta. Although this effect seems distant, it may already be impacting us in Oregon.

The study in Alberta noted that the tree line there has been steadily moving upward for the past forty years. As the timberline went up, the alpine meadows on the ridge tops became smaller, more crowded by the advancing forest, and more isolated. Populations of parnassius butterflies which once were able to migrate all along the ridge tops became isolated in meadows separated by the new stands of trees.

The researchers counted the number of butterflies in these isolated meadows. They found that over a period of ten years, the population levels became less and less synchronized. They

*The silverspot butterfly (*Speyeria callippe*) is federally endangered.*

concluded that the forest barriers kept the populations from interbreeding. This reduction in interbreeding leads to genetic impoverishment in small populations. The result is that the isolated populations are more vulnerable to local extinction.

In Oregon, the fragmentation of meadows due to climate change can be observed along coastal grassy headlands, in the Willamette Valley, and in both the Cascade Mountains and the Blue Mountains of Oregon. Although mostly a natural process, human impacts are factors in this process. In the Willamette Valley, for example, the first peoples regularly set fires to keep the valley grasslands open to enhance hunting for big game. The suppression of fire by European settlers would have resulted in fragmentation of the open grasslands even if the introduction of agriculture did not take place. Forests would have spread across much of the valley.

More recently, a little over a hundred years ago, the meadows of the Blue Mountains were kept open by vast herds of sheep. In the past half century, these meadows have begun to recover.

Grasses and other flowering plants have increased in vigor. Tree seedlings have also appeared on the edges of the meadows. The forests are on the march.

In the Cascades Mountains of Central Oregon the march of forests into meadows has been observed for some time. Unlike the situation in the alpine zone of the Rocky Mountains of Alberta, the timberline is not rising. In Alberta, the tree line is controlled by cold temperatures. In Oregon, a wetter, milder climate is allowing trees to take hold in meadows. There are many butterflies in addition to parnassius butterflies in our mountain meadows. As time goes on, we are likely to see butterfly populations become fragmented in isolated meadows. As the forest fills in small meadows, the stepping stones for recolonization will disappear. It appears probable that unchecked global warming will reduce the number of butterflies our descendants will see.

The march of the forests has started. Is it reasonable to hope our civilization will do what is necessary to control global warming?

The Owl and the Canary

When the Endangered Species Act (ESA) was passed in 1973, some people wondered why public funds should be spent to protect animals most people would never see. Who cares if a tree vole in Oregon goes extinct?

Scientists frequently used a "canary in the coal mine" analogy to help explain a significant aspect of endangered species protection. The analogy is based on the need for coal miners to detect dangerous levels of odorless carbon monoxide or methane. Contaminated air can kill miners before they sense the danger. Beginning in the early 1900's canaries were used as biological indicators of unsafe conditions in coal mine shafts. Canaries show distress when carbon monoxide or other toxic gases reach unsafe levels. If the canary fell off its perch, it was time to get out of the mine, pronto! In fact, canaries started swaying from side to side before they succumbed. As a result, they were better indicators of trouble than mice, which didn't show distress until they simply keeled over dead. Only in 1986 were the canaries replaced by electronic monitors.

The northern spotted owl became known as the canary in the coal mine for the old-growth ecosystems of the Pacific Northwest. The analogy was apt, because the health of spotted owl populations was clearly tied to the extent of old-growth forests. If the population of spotted owls was headed toward extinction, the entire old-growth ecosystem was obviously suffering. The owl was at the top of the food chain. If its numbers declined, the animals it fed on were probably declining, and the things they fed on in jeopardy. Lawsuits brought under the ESA led to the

Northwest Forest Plan (NFP). One of the primary objectives of the NFP was to set aside enough old growth forest to ensure the continued survival of the northern spotted owl.

Whether or not this action was sufficient to prevent continued decline of owl populations is an ongoing debate. Other threats to the northern spotted owl have arisen, such as displacement or genetic swamping by invasive barred owls. Because this has been in the news lately, it has deflected attention from the old growth forests. Here is where the "canary in the coal mine" analogy breaks down.

The timber industry has suggested that since the invasion of the barred owl has nothing to do with logging, protecting the northern spotted owl is moot and logging in old-growth forests should be resumed. Another suggestion has been that northern spotted owls might learn to live in habitats that don't quite qualify as old growth, or maybe even in "managed" stands of trees. Both of these approaches show a focus on the canary and not on the coal mine. The whole idea of taking canaries into the coal mine was to be assured the atmosphere in the mine was safe. It wouldn't do to fit little gas masks onto the canaries so they wouldn't suffer from toxic gasses. The idea is to keep the mine healthy, not simply to keep the canary healthy!

Remember the "canary, not the coal mine" fallacy when thinking about what you can do for the good of the natural world. It's my contention that the wisest place to put resources is in the preservation of natural systems. Organizations like The Nature Conservancy have a mandate to do just this. They don't just look for and protect endangered species. They use endangered species as canaries to help them locate ecosystems that are in trouble. Then they buy areas for preservation. If you are donating to an environmental cause, think twice about giving money to a wildlife park that claims to be preventing extinction by captive breeding. Captive breeding and cryogenic seed banks are fine. Their value is mostly in education. But they can't supplant the conservation of natural habitats where the endangered plants and animals live on their own.

The Secret of Sweet Maple Bud Soufflé

Thirty years ago I took a van load of students on a moss hunting expedition to Southwestern Oregon. We spent a couple of days on Veva Stansell's farm on the Pistol River near Gold Beach. Veva served as our guide, leading us to her favorite botanical haunts. She treated us to one of the best breakfasts we had on the trip.

The centerpiece of the breakfast was a delicious soufflé made with bigleaf maple flower buds. She had picked the buds early, just before they opened into an elongated flower cluster. When the bud scales were discarded, the undeveloped flower clusters looked like little broccoli tops. They were tender, sweet, and very tasty. I remember that breakfast every March, when the buds of Eugene's bigleaf maple swell and get ready to bloom.

Not long after that breakfast I tried collecting maple buds myself. I picked them at what I believed was the right stage and used them in a stir fry. Much to my dismay, the buds were not sweet at all. They were bitter. Thinking the problem was the process, I tried cooking them up as a frittata. This didn't help. Perhaps the buds were too far along? I tried another tree with buds in an earlier stage, not even splitting open yet. The results were much better; the buds were sweet. But another attempt demonstrated that gathering them at the right stage wasn't the whole story. Bitter buds again. The puzzle stayed with me, and I stopped cooking with maple blossoms until I learned about the unusual flowering pattern of the bigleaf maple.

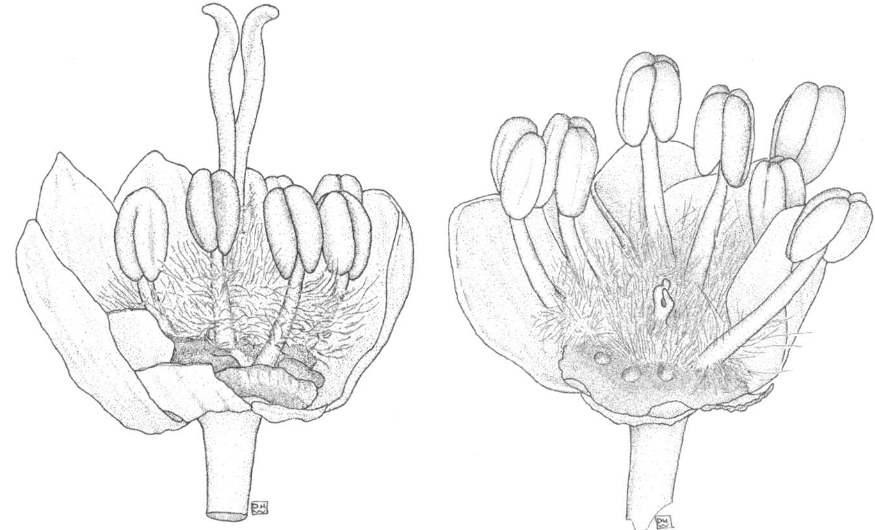

I discovered a secret about the sex life of bigleaf maples. They have two types of flowers: female (at left) and male (at right).

I finally discovered that bigleaf maples have two mating types. The first type, which I naturally call "Type I," is female first. When flower buds on Type I trees expand and blooming begins, only the female flowers open. The signs of first flowering on these trees are subtle, with only the forked stigmas sticking out of the flower clusters. The Type II trees are male first; when their flower clusters first expand it is easy to notice the fuzzy stamens offering pollen to bees and flies.

Both types of flowers, male and female, produce plenty of nectar to attract the flying insects that transfer pollen from stamens to stigmas. But the male flowers have an extra ingredient. Insect pollinated plants rely on sticky pollen. This allows clumps of pollen to stick to the legs of the visiting insects. Wind pollinated plants have dry pollen, so each pollen grain floats freely in the air. What makes pollen sticky? An oily substance produced in stamens just before the male flowers open. And, guess what? This oily pollen stick-um is very bitter. Aha!

Because flowers from Type I trees have female flowers developing first, only nectar is offered. Type II trees have male flowers producing nectar, too, but the overriding flavor comes from the oily stick-um for the pollen. So the secret to sweet maple bud soufflé is knowing what kind of tree to pick buds from. This is a bit tricky. It is not easy to tell Type I trees from Type II trees until the flower buds have opened. By that time the buds are too far along for culinary purposes.

What you need is some long-term planning. In spring, look closely at the first bloom of the maples on your walk route. The Type II trees are usually the first to bloom. They are the ones that are male first. Mark them with a mental big black X to signify "Do Not Eat." You might use a pocket knife to smooth a little bit of bark at knee level, where nobody else will notice, and write II with a Sharpie pen. Or do nothing at all. These are the trees you will avoid. When you find a tree that is female first, mark it inconspicuously with some notation that will remind you this is a Type I tree. Record it in a nature observation notebook.

Not every tree is a good one. It is important that it have low branches with flower clusters reachable from ground level. Two dozen clusters or so are needed for a good soufflé or stir fry. Plan, observe, and enjoy!

And now, since we're talking about tree sex, let's investigate vine maples. The breeding system for these shrubby trees is harder to observe than in bigleaf maples. I had to use a close-up lens to examine the critical features. Connie and I have two vine maples in our back yard. At the beginning of the flowering season, the first tree had young male flowers open and the second had young female flowers open. Pollen was carried by insects from the first to the second. The next week, the first tree had young female flowers on it and old male flowers. The second tree had young male flowers and old female flowers. The direction of pollen flow had reversed. Pollen was still going from young male to young female flowers, but now the second tree was providing pollen for the first.

Young male flowers have plump, unopened anthers. Old male flowers have anthers that have released all pollen. For me, the tricky part was to recognize the female flowers. They look as if they might be bisexual, with both stigmas and anthers. But the anthers are non-functional in the female flowers. Notice how in the old female flowers, marked by developing wings, the anthers are still unopened. With a hand lens, it should be possible to see this for yourself.

Honestly, I can't recommend trying to make a soufflé with vine maple buds. It's hard enough to recognize the right stuff on bigleaf maples. But with a little savvy about maple sex, you can still cook up a sweet breakfast.

Ranunculus glaberrimus *is a yellow buttercup native to the mountains of Southern Oregon.*

Fear

"I'd be way too scared to do that!"

That was the comment somebody once made when I mentioned how much I liked to go camping in the mountains. He said that having the dark woods around him would give him the creeps. What kind of thing might jump out of the dark and grab him? He would just sit there shaking in fear, jumping at every sudden sound. Unable to sleep, he'd be wide eyed and terrified until dawn. He couldn't feel comfortable at night without being in town, in a home with doors locked securely from the inside.

From time to time I have thought about how different my attitude is from his. I love to lie back under the stars, snuggling down into my sleeping bag, far away from any artificial light. I like to hug my knees in front of a campfire in the forest until sleepiness or the mosquitoes drive me into the tent. I feel comfortable in the wild.

The urban environment is what I don't trust. There's a certain unease I feel when in a town or city I don't know. Don't get me wrong—I enjoy travel. When I'm in a new city a little orientation usually suffices to set me happily exploring the sights. Being comfortable in the wild, however, is a different skill. It comes with long experience and frequent contact. Travel guides and maps are not going to suffice.

Fear of the unknown, or uncertainty about what to expect, is a part of outdoor life. When outdoorspeople get together, a common story topic is about moments of fear. It is as if, in hindsight, fear were a spice that keeps their senses sharpened and teaches lessons. A mountain climber once commented, "We tempt death to better understand life."

The most intense fear I can recall came from sudden, unexpected sounds. It is a common experience. In his autobiographical book, Winter Creek, Lane County author John Daniel wrote about his memories of fearful sounds. As a teenager, he found himself in the middle of a boulder field surrounded by the buzz of rattlesnakes. He was hiking alone in unfamiliar territory. His reaction was intense: "I remember feeling emptied of everything but my fear, my breathing." That is absolute fear, when there is nothing else in your body, the moment before you leap into action. It leaves a lasting memory.

The dark of a forest at night can inspire fear.

I have one experience that might match John Daniel's. I was also a teenager hiking alone, a few years older than he was at the time of his rattlesnake encounter. I was in familiar territory, the foothills of the Himalayas near my school, headed home after a long day's hike. I had been hunting butterflies in the valley twelve miles from home and didn't start home until it was getting dark. The middle four miles of the return trip were on a very narrow path across a steep hillside. It was a moonless night, and the path through the woods was so dark I had to feel my way along. I held the handle of my butterfly net ahead of me, tapping to feel for the edge of the trail. Luckily I had a big net with a five-foot handle.

My situation was dangerous because of the steepness of the

hillside. Had I walked off the edge, I would have tumbled a long way down. Instead of feeling fear, I focused my complete attention on being very, very careful. When I eventually I reached the main road, with four miles left to go, I felt considerable relief. I could increase my pace and be back in less than an hour.

Then I heard a strange sound: the loud thump of an animal jumping and landing on hard ground. It came from below the road, perhaps fifty or a hundred feet down the hillside. I stopped to listen carefully. It sounded like a large animal with padded feet. Tigers were unknown this high in the mountains, but it might be a leopard. After a few moments of silence, I heard rustling in the underbrush, moving across the hillside parallel to the road in the same direction I was headed. I began walking slowly again, more and more quickly, leaving the sound behind me. I heard nothing for a minute. Then I suddenly heard something running towards me from behind. That brought on a moment of absolute fear. I spun around with a scream, swinging my butterfly net at what I thought would be the height of a leopard's head.

The only thing I could see in the dark was some kind of motion about a foot off the ground. I screamed again, swinging the butterfly net back close to the ground.

Then, nothing. My screams echoed back to me across the canyon for a minute or more, one after another, bouncing off ridges farther and farther away. I stood in absolute silence, surrounded by darkness, still consumed by absolute fear, hair tingling on the back of my neck.

After an indeterminate time I turned and loped towards home. Probably the only thing behind me had been a leaf blowing in the wind. But there's no question that my fear had been absolute. Walking the rest of the way home I was a changed boy.

I'm sure that John Daniel would never recommend dancing across a boulder field with rattlesnakes underfoot, and I'd never recommend hiking alone in the mountains at night without a flashlight. What we experienced, however, has tempered our outlook on nature. Fear has helped us learn to feel at home in the wild.

Working Behind Enemy Lines

Cleaning out one of the back rooms in my shop, I took down a flutter of notes that had been taped to the wall over the desk where I used to work. The most recent was at least twelve years old. Humorous cartoons dominated, but there were also personal memorabilia, reminders of things to do, a few inspirational quotes, typing hints, and some mysterious clippings whose reason for saving are now lost to me.

One note struck me with strong emotional impact. It was a comment made by a college buddy who shared a room with me forty years ago. We have kept up with each other at least once every two or three years since we finished our undergraduate education. We knew each other as writers and activists, working together to protest the war in Vietnam. We marched and handed out leaflets together. We worked a printing machine together to publish our work and circulate the poems of our friends.

We went different ways, both in academic tracks, but in divergent disciplines. He taught writing, I taught botany. We shared a love of good writing that made it easy to maintain an active discussion of good things we read. He introduced me to the writing of Primo Levi, the Italian chemist and Holocaust survivor. I put in his hands on a copy of Richard Rhodes' *The Making of the Atomic Bomb.*

What was pinned to my wall was the phrase, "I've been working behind enemy lines for years." It was a comment made in a telephone conversation around 1990, while he was explaining how he made his writing students think for themselves. They should write well, and to do that should be ready to question dogma and rebel against rigid notions. This is not military activity, it is intellectual combat. It is as real within a country as it is serious between countries. In the 1960s there was a debate over whether or not it was more effective to drop out and resist the system or to join and subvert. An English teacher who worked for a public institution and urged his students to think independently could be labeled an enemy of the establishment, somebody who was "working behind enemy lines."

Considering the real wars that governments wage, it might seem fatuous to suggest there are battles being fought without weapons. But so it is in the environmental field.

When public lands are under the political administration of advocates of resource exploitation, it is subversive to promote preservationist principles. Environmentalists working for the Bureau of Land Management or the U.S. Forest Service often find themselves in this awkward position, as if they are working behind enemy lines. They chose forestry or botany or wildlife biology as careers because they love the wild. A career in natural science seemed a most proper career. However, mandates on how to manage public lands are not consistent from one administration to another. The conservation of our natural resources depends on the quiet work of career naturalists, just as peaceful relations with other countries depends on career diplomats.

It grieves me to read general derogatory comments aimed at "the Forest Service" or "the BLM" in conservationist writings. The implication is that all employees of an agency are to blame for poorly thought-out policies advocated by administrators of the agency, administrators who are political appointees. It is unfair to color all with the same brushstroke. Just as we can support the troops without supporting a war, we must support the biologists, geologists, and other front-line scientists while opposing the policies of their agency's administrative heads. It is important to take time to acknowledge and give proper credit to the protectors of nature who are working behind enemy lines.

Looking Up to Find Your Way

I sometimes spend part of October at a ranch on the Modoc Plateau in northwestern California. One of the wonderful things about this juniper and ponderosa highland is the clarity of the sky at night. One year we arrived the evening of the full moon. What a glorious welcome when the mystic golden disc rose over the piney ridge. As the days passed, the moon rose later and later, so that in the hours just before dawn the bright moon was still high in the sky. My friends and I treasured this phase of the moon during our high school hiking days. We could get up in the wee hours of the morning and not need flashlights to begin our hikes. The bright moon high in the western sky would light our way until the sun brightened the eastern sky.

Orion, the hunter, has a starry sword hanging from his three-star belt.

On towards the new moon (a strange name for no moon), the night sky was dazzling in the absence of the moon. The first time I looked up at a moonless Modoc sky I was frustrated at how hard it was for me to find the Big Dipper and the North Star. It was disorienting to be lost in the sky because of too many stars! In town the sky is so obscured with urban light pollution that only bright stars of constellations like Ursa Major (the Big Dipper) and Cassiopeia really stand out. Eventually, I learned to recognize the proper parts of the sky above the ranch. Late in the year the Big Dipper is so low in the sky that it can be lost in the northern horizon's haze. The "Big W," my personal name for the stars of Cassiopeia, is on the opposite side of the North Star from the Big Dipper. Once I've found the North Star, all is well.

Walking at night on a clear starry night in Modoc is a real treat. It has been a long time since I have been in a place where the skies are so clear that the stars alone are enough to provide light to walk by. It helps to have a dark road bordered by swards of pale, dry grass. Unlike stepping out in the moonlight, hiking by starlight takes a little time for adjustment. I recall the part of Richard Rhodes' *The Making of the Atomic Bomb* where he describes Rutherford and his assistants sitting in pitch darkness, telling jokes and playing word games until their eyes were so adapted to the dark that they could see the faint flashes of atomic particles hitting a fluorescent screen. It took about twenty minutes of walking before I was really comfortable hiking by starlight. Fortunately, on the Modoc Plateau there are so few cars that none came by to spoil my accommodation to the dark.

A friend recently explained how she can tell which way is south in autumn, even on an overcast day. The sun is low enough in fall that the daytime sky is always brightest in the south. I replied that the best time to track a compass direction for cross country travel is when the sun is low and bright. I use the compass to determine the direction I want to go, then I note which direction trees are casting shadows. While I walk, I simply make sure the tree shadows keep pointing at the same angle. That makes it easy to keep walking in the right direction without constantly pulling the compass out of my pocket.

Forever Young

As I age, I have been thinking about buds. Dormant winter buds are one of the important differences between plants and animals. Of course there is the obvious difference that animals can move around and plants can't. Plants have different ways to compensate for being sessile–attached to a surface. In our climate, getting through the winter presents a challenge to all beings. Some plants simply live as annuals, using their seeds to weather out hard times. Many insects and other invertebrates overwinter in a similar fashion, as eggs or resistant pupae. When it comes to dealing with winter cold, long-lived animals either keep themselves warm with an insulating covering or seek out protected spots to hibernate. Perennial plants have to withdraw into underground bulbs and rhizomes or develop winter buds to protect their sensitive growing tissue.

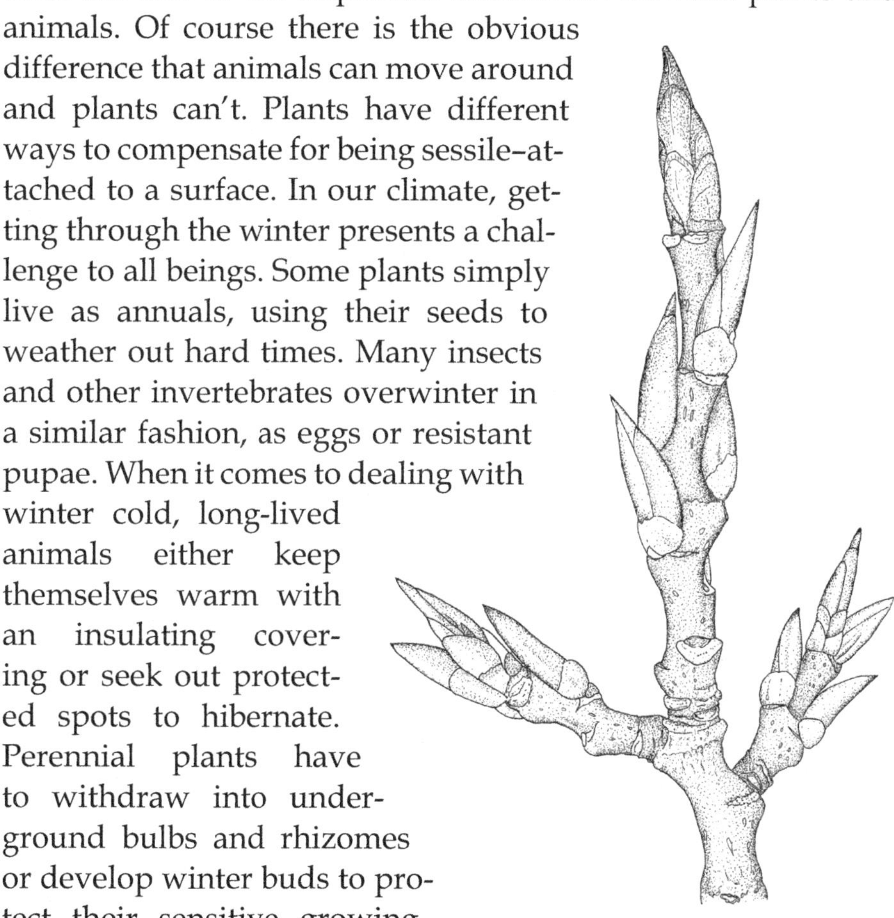

The buds of black cottonwood trees grow slowly throughout the winter.

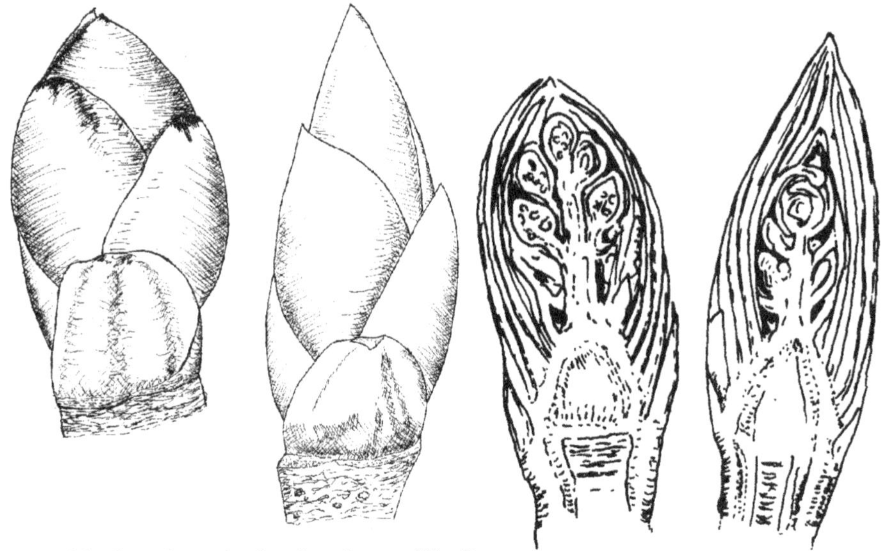

Inside the winter buds of osoberry ("Indian plum"), new shoots are growing from the eternally young meristem.

The winter buds of trees and shrubs have my special attention in winter because they are constantly in my face as I tramp through the woods. Winter buds actually begin developing early in the summer. While leaves are gathering energy for wood, flowers, and fruit, they are also building buds as an investment in the next season. Buds can form either at the tip of a shoot or in the angle between leaf stalk and stem. The buds are wrapped in bud scales—tough, durable modifications of leaves. The scales not only keep predators and pathogens from getting at the tender kernel inside, but they also keep the kernel from drying out.

It is that tender kernel that contains the primary meristem of the plant. Meristem is a term for stem tissue—undifferentiated cells that are forever young. When you cut open a bud with a razor blade, you often see little knobs and stalks that will develop into leaves and flowers. These are called primordia. Primordia develop from the meristem.

Embryonic animals have stem tissue that is as versatile as the meristem, with unlimited growth potential. But as animals age the only stem tissue they retain is limited to replacing specific cells, such as in the skin. We adults do not have anything like a meristem. The meristem can produce all parts of a plant. Meristems are not found just in buds. Woody plants have a sheet-like meristem that envelops their shoots and produces the annual layers of wood. When the meristems die, the plant dies. But as long as the meristem is preserved, an individual plant can grow indefinitely. That's why there are plants that are thousands of years old.

Take a moment to let the wonder of this sink in. Plants contain the secret of eternal life. We walk on the mosses and liverworts of the forest floor. Some people might consider these to be lowly species. But unlike us, they contain the elixir of youth.

They are forever young.

Index

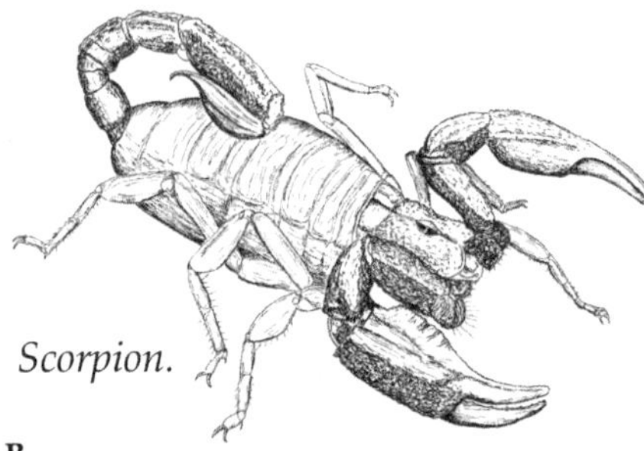
Scorpion.

Western gull.

Sword fern.

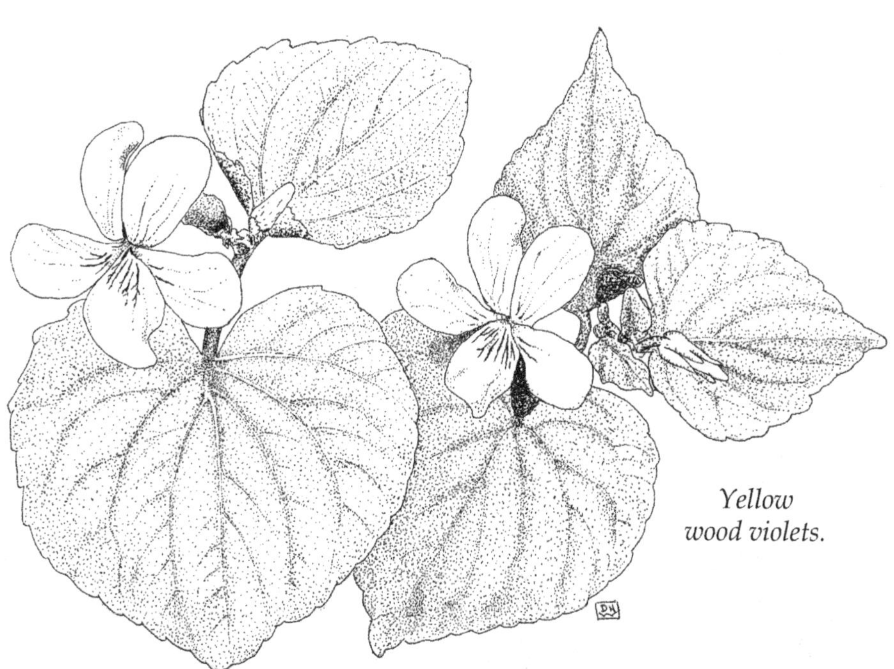

Yellow wood violets.

Sandhill crane.

Made in the USA
Middletown, DE
27 May 2024